T0248039

Keep Living

Keep Living

LOREAL CHANEL "LC" PALMER

Post Hill
PRESS

A POST HILL PRESS BOOK

ISBN: 979-8-88845-084-0
ISBN (eBook): 979-8-88845-085-7

Cover design by Jim Villaflores
Cover photo by Dalvin Adams
Interior design and composition by Greg Johnson, Textbook Perfect

This is a work of nonfiction. All people, locations, events, and situations are portrayed to the best of the author's memory.

Post Hill Press
New York • Nashville
posthillpress.com

Published in the United States of America
1 2 3 4 5 6 7 8 9 10

This book is dedicated to my three beautiful children,
who remind me daily that miracles really do happen.

Thank you, Alexander, for being your intelligent little self daily;
your sensitive and sensible nature never ceases to amaze me,
and I know you'll change the world.

Thank you, Alexandra, for reminding me that seeing things
differently is a superpower; you remind me so much of myself,
and I promise to nurture your kindness and curiosity.

Thank you, Aaliyah, for being unapologetically yourself 24/7;
you know what you want and you go for it—keep doing that!

Contents

Foreword
by Keke Palmer

There is nothing quite like having a big sister; she's the one who came before you, who was with you from the very beginning, the keeper of countless inside jokes, secrets, and memories and is someone who always has your back...well, if you're lucky enough to have that kind of big sister, and I am definitely one of the lucky ones.

As you may have already figured out, our family is tight; we love big, work hard, defend one another to the core, and always stick together. Growing up, Loreal and I had different strengths. She was considered quieter and more reserved, and I was considered more extroverted, but the gag is, neither of us fit in one box. My sister is beautifully complex.

I've always been inspired by her thirst for knowledge, her passion for great literature and horror films (she's the one who introduced me to the movie, *Candyman* and the reason I didn't sleep for a week—thanks, Sis!). I admire the loyalty and creativity she brings to her family and friends, and into all situations. And now, I particularly admire her ability to step out into the unknown and open up even when it's really hard. In the midst of a sea of change in circumstances, Loreal chose to live her life to the fullest and to continue to write her own story...the story that she deserves. She went back to school to get her Master's degree and is now pursuing her PhD. She challenged herself to appear on *Claim to Fame*, and won the whole damn thing! America got to see what we've always known about Loreal and of course, they fell in love with her.

As a new inductee to the most sacred club of motherhood, I've been thinking a lot about the women who come before us and the wisdoms they share with each passing generation—a beautiful intergenerational network of knowledge. In this book, Loreal shares many of those powerful wisdoms from our own grandmothers, our spectacular mama, as well as what Loreal has gleaned along the way.

In sharing her story, Loreal gives voice to a lot of beautiful and inspiring revelations, and I can't wait for you to go on the journey with her.

I've witnessed my sister go through fire and come through the other side with grace, strength, and, yes, humor. When many people would lay down, she got up. I know this book will impact lives; inspiring people to change what's not working in order to live in fulfilled purpose and true happiness. Loreal is a testament to the fact that it is never too late to start fresh and that sometimes unexpected road bumps can be gifts from the universe.

A flood of memories came rushing back when I read this book. I was reminded of the strength of our family, the many memories we've made, and of the fact that everything we've shared from childhood on has gotten us to who we are and where we are now.

I've had a front row seat to Loreal's transformation from the kind, and sometimes naïve girl (I say it with love) in her twenties to the beautiful, empowered woman in her thirties and you better believe that I'm staying tuned for what's next and you should too. So, without further ado, Baby, this is Loreal Palmer, and her book *Keep Living!*

Introduction

"Are you gay?" These three little words would make all the difference to thirty-two-year-old me. They would burst the safe little marital bliss bubble that I had spent the better part of ten years creating, and would thrust me into a place that I had spent my entire life trying to avoid: a place of discomfort. Divorce is stressful enough on its own, listed second only to the death of a spouse as the most stressful life event one can endure. But imagine going through a divorce, and realizing that you don't really know who *you* are. You have to deal with emotions and logistics and then you look around and see what you're left with, and I thought I was left with *nothing*.

Nothing, metaphorically of course, because our arrangement was actually rather fair and amicable. Mentally and emotionally, however, I was a ball of confusion: Who am I if I'm not a wife? I'm still a mom, but what *kind* of mom am I? Do I still just do everything exactly the same way I did as a wife? For so long, I had attached my identity to those surrounding me. I was the daughter of Larry and Sharon; the sister of Lauren, Lawrence, and Lawrencia; the mom of Ali, Liyah, and AJ; and my most important role to date, the wife of

Frank. I knew who I was to all of these people, but who was I to myself? I didn't know. I remember sitting there with myself one day after the divorce process had begun, trying to imagine my future, and I couldn't. I literally could not for the life of me imagine an existence post-divorce. I couldn't envision what life without Frank would look like, even though I had obviously existed pre-Frank. I just couldn't see the possibility of an existence post-him.

No one enters a relationship anticipating its end; we're all expecting a happily ever after, but what happens when your version of happily ever after clashes with your reality? What if your happily ever after had never been rooted in reality to begin with? Frank had been my first kiss, my first sexual experience, my first love, but was that love the kind of love I wanted it to be? These were the questions I'd have to ask myself as I went down the divorce rabbit hole. I slowly came to the realization that what I had been mourning wasn't necessarily the romantic end of our relationship, but the end of a strong companionship. Who would I watch Food Network with? Who would I watch my B horror movies with? Who would I bother on my road trips? This line of questioning, of course, led me down an entirely new rabbit hole. Did I *really* ever *love* Frank? The answer was of course I did, but maybe not like a typical wife loves a husband. Maybe this had just been a platonic love all along.

Frank was and still is my best friend. Over ten years, there wasn't much I didn't know about him. The one thing I didn't know, however, would eventually be our undoing. When Frank came out to me, he asked me to continue our marriage. So I dove into research on mixed-orientation marriages, that's what they're called, and found that the ones that were successful usually involved couples well into their sixties. In our early thirties, the odds were not in our favor. The average length of time a mixed-orientation marriage lasted from coming out to divorcing for our age group was two years. Two years? Not knowing who I was without him yet, I was determined to beat those odds. We could make this work; we *would* make this work.

We couldn't make this work. The thought of an open marriage seemed okay, given the alternative, but putting it into practice did nothing but convince me that we just weren't going to work. I downloaded Tinder, while he downloaded Grindr. He went on dates almost every single day of the week. I planned dates, then ghosted the poor men. I couldn't do this. The more I tried, the lower my self-esteem became. What was wrong with me? Why couldn't I go out there and sleep with men who clearly wanted to sleep with me? I was definitely missing that physical aspect of our relationship, so why was I unable to go out there and get it? I was asking the wrong questions. Why couldn't I see that my husband not wanting to sleep with me was the actual problem here? I don't mean him being gay. Being gay wasn't a problem in and of itself. The problem was us thinking that we could be happy in a heterosexual relationship while one of us wasn't heterosexual. It wasn't going to work. It was never going to work. But why did I want it to work? Why did I *need* it to work? That was simple—because I'm the peacemaker.

Anyone with multiple siblings knows that we all play a different role in the family. Keke is the friendly, outgoing empath. Lawrencia is the bossy, spoiled one (we love you Rennie). Lawrence is the stoic, yet ridiculously hilarious one, and I'm the one who everyone counts on to keep the peace when the other personalities clash. I'm the big sister, and apparently I had extended that role outside of my family of origin and into the very way I saw myself existing within the world. I became this peacemaker for everyone and everything, and now I had become the peacemaker in my marriage. The more chaotic it became, the more peace I tried to spread. You know those memes where the world is literally exploding and the caption reads: "It's fine. I'm fine." Those are based on me. I was always okay and always fine...if always actually means never, or if fine and okay mean down bad.

I have never liked stress. No one does, of course, but I would go out of my way to avoid a situation that even hinted at potentially raising my blood pressure (yes, little kid me was worried about her blood pressure). Other kids at the park when I went? Avoid. Raising my hand in class when I absolutely knew the answer? Avoid. And when I couldn't successfully avoid the discomfort, I would always walk away feeling like this was the absolute worst thing that could ever happen to me in my entire life.

When I was younger, my grandma Mildred had a saying that all her children and grandchildren would hear time and time again. Whenever one of us declared that the worst possible thing ever had happened (all the way from "I forgot my line in the play" to "someone stole my new purse on the bus"), her response was always the same: *Keep living.* That's it, that was her grand advice. A smirk, maybe a chuckle thrown in, and a "keep living." As a kid, I paid it little attention; she was old, and back then old people never made sense when I didn't want them to. Instead of dissecting what it meant, I would dismiss it as Grandma being Grandma. As I got older, though, it made all the sense in the world. The longer you live, the more you will experience. Some of it will be really good, some of it will be really bad, but you have to keep living in order to find out which one it'll be.

This book chronicles my many attempts to keep living. There are moments that happen in here that truly felt like the worst thing I could've ever imagined happening to me, but things would only go on to get worse! But then they would also get better...and then worse again. I'm told that "tragic serenity" (thank you Shane) is the term for accepting the unpredictable ebb and flow of life. That it's this place of being at peace with the fact that life is in constant flux and that at any moment things can go extremely right or extremely wrong, and the only way to find out is to basically keep existing. That's a scary thought, but I suppose it's also comforting.

Think about it. The best thing that we can do at any point in our life is to keep living it—that's it. Whatever the experience may be, you go through it and make it out on the other side. I had gotten *really* good at navigating around my negative experiences, choosing instead to dance around them in hopes of some magical fairy popping out of the sky and making it all better. I was afraid to accept that whatever was going on was simply my journey; it was a *moment* in my journey. Yes, some moments were longer than others, and hurt so much worse than others, and often I dealt with back-to-back-to-back *worse* periods. But they would get better...then worse...then okay... then not too bad— I didn't die. I just had to keep living.

1

Pilot

You know how on the first day of school, when your teacher says, "Okay, boys and girls, we're going to go around the class and get to know each other," you have to tell everyone your name, age, and one word that describes *you*? Well, my name is Loreal, I'm thirty-four, and the word that best describes me is fearful, but I suppose you could also say anxious. I like to psychoanalyze myself from time to time, to attempt to access the most recessive parts of my brain and locate the precise incident that caused my anxiety. It would be awesome if I could now share that moment with you, but I can't. I haven't located that file yet, or maybe it doesn't exist. Maybe it's genetic.

My grandmother, Mildred Davis, was the most amazing woman to ever exist on planet Earth; I'm ready to argue about it. She grew up in Oxford, Mississippi, during the 1930s. After completing college at the age of sixteen, she moved to Chicago during the great migration of Black people from the South to the North. She opened her own hair salon on Chicago's West Side that lasted for over forty years. During the race riots, her shop was burned down, and she rebuilt. When she was in her mid-thirties, she was in a horrific car accident in which she severely injured her back. She and the car were thrown into a ditch, and she was afraid that no one would see her down there, so she crawled out just enough that someone, anyone, would see her. The doctors were in awe of the fact that she was even able to *move*.

When my mom, Sharon, was ten, her father died of lung cancer. When she came home from school that day, my grandmother delivered the news to her and her twin sister, Karen. She hugged them and said, "I want you to know that your way of living will not change." It didn't. Her house was paid off by the time my mother completed high school, and even after my grandmother's arthritis forced her to close shop, she still did hair from the kitchen of her suburban home for her most loyal customers. I would wake up on Saturday mornings after spending the night and smell the hot comb or perm. I could tell who the customer was based on the smell of the treatment. I was always happiest when it was Miss Lucille—Miss Lucille came bearing gifts. My grandmother had seven children, twenty grandchildren, and too many great-grand-children to sit here and pretend to count. She was strong, and she was fierce, but she was also *scary*.

Fearful, anxious, scary. No matter the word, they all have the same meaning in this book. I use fearful because it's what sounds right to me. Anxiety is what society calls it today, and scary is what my grandmother called it when she saw it in me and made me promise to fight it. I remember in third grade, I wanted to sing in the talent show. Pocahontas was my favorite movie at the time, and although my family identifies solely as Black, I was made aware that we had Native American and Irish roots as well. So my mom made a really big deal out of me performing "Colors of the Wind" from the Disney movie in the talent show. She was very serious about practice. After school, she would have me sing the song to her over and over again. My voice was fine, but when I performed I resembled a deer in headlights—the rehearsals were for that. She thought that the more I sang, the more familiar it'd become, and the less afraid I'd be. She made me sing that damn song in front of anyone who would listen.

One day after school, she took me to my grandmother's house to sing it for her. As I stood there in my grandmother's kitchen, standing as straight as a toothpick, avoiding eye contact, choosing instead to belt my heart out to the micro- wave, not letting even a fingertip slip out of the invisible box of safety I'd created for myself, my mom started her coaching. "You have to look at us when you sing, Lori. Don't just stand there looking scared. Is you scared?" I shook my head no as my eyes were too afraid to even blink. "Are. You. Scared?" She said it in the softest voice, but it wasn't sweet. It was that tone every kid knows is a warning, but outsiders wouldn't be able to pick up on.

She wanted me to answer out loud.

You weren't allowed to be quiet in my family. Number one, it was disrespectful not to respond verbally when an adult asked you a question. Number two, my grandmother just always demanded we speak up. You can't be heard if you don't speak up. She would say, "I don't like no measly-mouthed kids—just starin' and lookin'." Then she'd make this face where she'd buck her teeth out like a beaver and open her eyes

3

real wide, as if that's what quiet children look like. (It's funny, thinking about it now, the face looked exactly like that meme with the seal staring disproportionately into the camera that reads, "Kids be like: You got games on your phone?" Perhaps she was on to something.)

"I- I'm not scared," I stuttered out. It was true, I wasn't scared—I was *petrified*. I could sing in front of my grand-mother day in and day out, but my mother was another story. She represented a real audience. Her criticism would be swift and honest. Grandma would smile and say, "Beautiful," as she cackled and clapped with her hands, knotted from the arthritis—even if it were anything but beautiful. My mother, however, was a performer. Her high school years were spent in the drama club. She was competitive in speech and worked for years as an actress in Chicago's Black Ensemble Theater. She loved telling the story about how she performed in *The Other Cinderella* for its entire run while nine months pregnant with me. Years later, after my grandmother passed away, I would find a box full of awards and newspaper articles praising my mom's performances. My grandmother had kept them so long that the pages had started to yellow, but she *kept* them. And she did so in a place that was so personal and private so that she could revisit them whenever she needed to. I now keep them in a similar place.

Performing is what my mom knew; what she both loved and lived, and what she knew as I was practicing "Colors of the Wind" is that whatever it was that I was doing was *not* it.

My mother wasn't big on shopping and girls' trips, but practicing for a performance was something that brought us together. We both had a love for creativity, and she saw that love in me long before I saw it within myself. She also saw

4

that I was scary, and in her own way she wanted to break me of that; you never get anywhere by being afraid of everywhere. She sighed and placed her hands on her knees, as she always did before a speech. "I can't want this for you. I can't get up there and perform for you. You look afraid, and no one wants to see you up there singing, afraid. If you wanna sing, then sing, dammit. If you don't, stop wasting our time."

My grandmother scrunched her face up and folded her hands together, the piece of paper towel she'd often clutch smashed between the two. "Let her 'lone, Sharon. Just let her 'lone. She doin' alright." She shot me a smile full of pity, and I felt my eyes begin to water.

I did want to sing, I love to sing to this day, but I do get scared when it's in front of people. I didn't know how to respond at that moment, so I cried. "Stop all that cryin', nobody did nothing to you," my mom snapped. My mother loves us very much, but she is not an affectionate woman. My crying made her uncomfortable, because she didn't know how to stop it. She was from a family of ambitious go-getters who didn't respond well to emotional outbursts.

My grandmother got up from her chair and shooed my mom away. She whispered, but I could hear her—perhaps that was her intent. "Just go on out front for a minute," she motioned as she shooed her to the front of the house. My mom got up, huffing and sucking her teeth like a grumpy teenager, and made her way out of the kitchen.

When she was gone, my grandmother started inching towards me, until she stood directly in front of me. Her 5'5" frame looked at me with concern, and I looked back at her just...watching me. Her light brown hair pulled back into a ponytail, complete with homemade clip-in bangs, her white

Taylor Family Reunion T-shirt, and brown leggings hidden beneath her brown apron. When she finally spoke, she said, "Whatchu scared of?" I started to shrug, but then remembered I didn't want to be a measly-mouthed kid. "I don't know." She sighed. "You can't be scared of stuff, Loreal." The pronunciation sounding like Luh-ri-el. "Don't be scary. I was scary, and it stopped me from doing a lot of things. Being scary don't pay. You make the wrong decisions being scary. If you wanna sang, then sang. If you don't, then don't. But don't not sang because you too scared." I heard her, but not really. I had decades of scary, wrong decisions to come.

On the drive home, my mom didn't say anything. When we got in the house, I went straight to my room and laid in my bed. I didn't even bother to remove my coat or shoes. As I started to fall asleep, my mom came in and sat at my feet. "I didn't mean to yell at you. You're just really talented, and I don't want you to be afraid." My eyes began to water for the second time that day. "What are you afraid of?" There was that question again, and I genuinely didn't have an answer. What the hell *was* I afraid of? "Maybe it's seeing the people looking at you? You sing alone all the time. Maybe try taking your glasses off." I have always been as blind as a bat without my glasses, seeing up to roughly six inches in front of my face without them.

I got up off my bed and made my way to the center of my room, coat and shoes still on. I took my glasses off and closed my eyes. *Okay, Loreal, you can't even see. So if somebody laughs at you, you won't even know.* There it was—that's what I had been afraid of. No one had ever laughed at me singing before; in fact, everyone had always loved my voice when they'd stumbled upon me singing. Why did I think they would laugh? I opened my mouth, and I sang. I looked around and when the reality that I couldn't really make out my mother's position in the room, let alone her face, hit, I felt this rush of relief. I started to move my hands dramatically in places where I felt it'd be effective. I took a few steps forward, one big one back when I hit the chorus. My previously paralyzed limbs now had movement. When it was me singing alone, I was no longer Loreal, I was *Pocahontas*. As the bridge finished and the final chorus built up, I remember extending my arm out reaching for the "blue corn moon," and rubbing my forearms as I sang the words "copper skinned." It was dramatic for sure, but it was a *performance*. I finished and put my glasses back on just in time to see my mom rushing for me, smiling. "Yes, Lori! Yes!" She squeezed me tight and swayed us both from side to side. I felt good, and I felt accomplished, but what I didn't realize was that I had just placed a bandage on the problem. I didn't address this irrational fear; I simply avoided it, and just like the decades of wrong decisions, I'd also have decades of avoidance ahead of me.

I'll spare you the boring details, but the talent show went fine. It was the first of many in which I'd take my glasses off to perform. In fact, I'd become a regular soloist in both the winter and spring school performances by the seventh grade at St. Benedict Catholic Elementary School in Blue Island, Illinois. I wasn't from Blue Island, though. That was a nice area. I was from Robbins, Illinois. Mudville stand up! We called it Mudville because the town used to be so impoverished that there were no sidewalks, so when it rained, everything became mud. Most of the kids in my class lived in Blue Island; there was one other Black girl who lived in Robbins and even went to my church, but we didn't really talk. One day during lunch, a boy told me, "We drove through Robbins the other day, and my mom said it's full of drugs and gangbangers. Isn't that where you live, Loreal?" I didn't know if he wanted to be offensive, or if he was generally inquisitive, so I just said "yup" and continued eating.

Robbins wasn't a nice area, not when I lived there. It was once a blossoming town established by middle-class Black people looking for their own piece of suburbia. It was far enough from the hustle and bustle of Chicago life, but close enough when you yearned that excitement. It is the second-oldest Black town in the North and gave birth to the nation's first Black-owned airport. I don't know where it went wrong, but by the time I lived there, nothing was blossoming; on some streets the grass didn't even want to be there. The airport was long gone, and the only businesses that thrived were liquor stores, an urban nook called Manny's Blue Room, and a J&J's Fish. For everything else we had to drive to one of the next towns over—the white towns—of Midlothian or Crestwood. They didn't want us there, and they had no problem making it known. In my mother's day, they would throw rocks at them as they attempted to walk home. We didn't get things thrown at us, but we were watched.

Once when I was fourteen, a cousin and I wanted to walk to Walgreens to get makeup. We were in high school now, and we had to look the part. We made it there just fine, and purchased our glosses and eyeliner, and began the walk back home. We were waiting at the crosswalk when two middle-aged white men pulled up beside us in their pickup and yelled out, "Get back to Robbins, niggers!" And sped off. My cousin and I just looked at one another with our mouths wide open. Then we laughed. Maybe it was nerves, but we were stunned by the utter ridiculousness of it all. What were they seeking to gain in this instance? Two obviously grown men, wanting to call two obviously young teenage girls niggers, and then speed off. Were we supposed to be offended? Afraid? I mean, yeah, it sucked, and later I realized just how horribly that could've gone if they *hadn't* sped off, but if their goal was to make us feel uncomfortable, it didn't work. By this age we had already grown accustomed to being the *other* of society. I was used to being the *other* in general.

I've always been the *other*. I was the only Catholic of my cousins—I was also the only one who went to church, period, outside of Easter; I was the only Black girl in my friend group, and I was the only girl on my block who just did not fit in. From a young age, I'd been learning to dance between two worlds. I'm pretty damn good at it now, but back then it was rough. School Loreal hadn't quite figured out how to turn it off when she came back home. Some of my cousins would ask my mom, "Why she talk white?" When I'd venture outside of my house, the neighborhood boys would always seem to be right out there waiting for me, "Hey, white girl! Where you goin', white girl? You wanna be white so bad. You're too ugly to be a white girl; they don't want you." They would follow me the entire walk to my grandmother's house, and depending on the type of day I'd had, sometimes I'd powerwalk so that they couldn't catch up and see the tears that had begun to sting my eyes.

One day, I arrived at my grandmother's house and as soon as I entered her door, the tears came rushing. Her smile turned into a frown as she asked me what was wrong. I could barely breathe, so I don't know how she got this: *Those boys were teasing me as I tried to walk to your house*, from this:

Th—buh—ME, walkin' house. She had just made some Jell-O, so she sat me down in the kitchen and made me a bowl. Then she told me a story. When she was a little girl, they learned in a schoolhouse. She said every day she would bring a shiny red apple to school, and every day a little boy would eat her apple. She cried the first time, then, after the next few times, she was resigned to the fact that she was basically bringing the apple for him. At some point she grew tired, and when he went to take a bite of her apple, she balled her fist up as tight as she could, and she hit him in his face as hard as she could. "Mildred!" Her schoolteacher called out. "It's about damn time!"

It was about damn time for me too. I was inspired by my grandmother's story, perhaps that was her reason for telling it, but I was so sick and tired of being afraid to leave the house. I started my walk home, this time hoping to see the boys. They didn't disappoint. They followed me all the way through the vacant lot behind my grandmother's house, past the duplex that led to my block, Kedvale Avenue, and all the way to my front yard. A few nights before, lightning had struck a tree in my backyard, and knocked a big branch off next to our shed. I was headed straight for that branch.

I picked it up and stomped back to my front yard. One of the boys noticed me, "What are you doing?" He looked worried. Good.

"If you don't get off my property, I'm gonna hit you," I said, eerily calm.

"With a stick?" His eyes grew wide.

Before I could answer, my dad came peeking his head through the front door. My parents' bedroom faced our front yard; I'd overlooked this. The tears came, betraying my feigned confidence. "They keep teasing me, Dad. Every day, and I'm tired of it."

He frowned. "So what are you planning to do with that stick?"

I didn't hesitate. "I'ma beat they ass."

I had never cursed in front of my father before. That was a huge no-no, but considering the circumstances, he let it slide. He walked all the way outside of the front door, letting the screen slam behind him. "Gimme the stick," he said facing me. I reluctantly gave it to him. Then he faced the boys, "Listen here, you guys are gonna stop messing with my daughter. You hear me? I know all y'all parents, and if we have to have this conversation again, we'll have it with them. Y'all hear me?" The boys nodded in unison.

My dad turned back into the house, and as I followed him in, one of the boys yelled, "Loreal!" I turned around silently, defeated and embarrassed. "You going inside?"

I responded with an annoyed, "Yeah." He looked confused. "Why? The sun still out." Now I was confused. "You don't even like me!" I shot back.

"I do like you," he said. "We just be playin'."

That day was probably my first official day of merger training. I would play with my school friends during the day, and on weekends and during summers I'd play with my neighborhood friends. They'd share what public school was like, and I'd share what private school was like. For the first time, being in the middle of two worlds wasn't a weakness, but a strength. I was learning to be adaptive. But by the time I had successfully adapted, it would be time to adapt again, and on and on that pattern would repeat for decades....

2

Girl Meets World

I hated birthdays growing up. Let me rephrase that: I hated birthday *parties* growing up. It's not that I didn't like attending parties, I actually loved *going* to parties—I just didn't like the stress of throwing one of my own. Remember how I mentioned I was "scary"? Well, here's a perfect example of that. The thought of throwing a party made me anxious. I would stress over whether or not people would show up, and if they *did* show up, whether or not they would have a good time. Even as a kid this worried me, so when I turned eleven on a random weekday, it was the perfect excuse *not* to have a party. This predates rapper ILoveMakonnen going up on a Tuesday.

My dad always made a huge deal of birthdays when we were growing up. He would make us feel like royalty. We basically got a king-for-a-day pass; whatever we said (within reason) was law. For this particular birthday, I had spent weeks crafting the perfect day. I wanted to stay home from school, but that wasn't going to fly (within reason, remember), but once I got home I could do whatever I wanted. So what did I want, you ask? I wanted my dad to make my favorite dinner: mashed potatoes, cream corn, broccoli (his idea, not mine), fried pork chops, and honey biscuits. Then we would do cake and candles—he would bake whatever cake I requested, which was yellow with vanilla frosting. After we would all get fat and happy, we would watch a family movie of my choosing.

I spent the entire school day daydreaming about my birthday celebration. My sister, Keke, would have to let me watch whatever I wanted on TV today, because it was my birthday. A week before Christmas, we'd gotten a satellite dish, and I had become obsessed with the Disney Channel. I had a small VHS collection of Disney Channel Original Movies (DCOMS, as we '90s kids affectionately refer to them) I had recorded, which were my prized possessions, along with my Mariah Carey high school reunion special. Maybe we'd just watch those since we both loved them—I wasn't a complete jerk, after all.

I *ran* out of school that day; couldn't get to my mom's car fast enough. Everyone was in my way. Even the crossing guard was taking his sweet time, crawling into the middle of the street and raising his sign oh so painstakingly slow. On the other side of the street, my mom was waiting for me in the parking lot. I could see her flashing her perfect rows of teeth, smiling as she waved me over to her. I skipped my way over, jumping into her arms as she squeezed me tight, peppering me with kisses. "Moooooom!" I whined as I wiped the wetness from my face. I didn't like getting kisses, which meant she loved giving them to me.

We got into the car, and as I buckled myself in, I saw her adjust the rearview mirror so that she could look at me in the

13

backseat. "Girl, what is we watching tonight?!" she asked, purposely trying to sound "cool." It made me smile. "I don't know yet." I really didn't know. Choosing a movie has always been serious business for me. Going to Blockbuster was an event. I'd go in knowing exactly what I wanted to watch (usually a horror movie), then I'd walk down every aisle, enchanted by the covers of all the movies I'd never heard of. Just like that, forty minutes would go by while my parents sat in the car waiting for me to come back out and announce it was time to pay. When I got older, they'd just give me the card. Tonight, I really wanted to watch *Lost Boys*, but we'd all already seen that movie too many times. And anyway, this was a special occasion. A repeat viewing, even if it *was* a classic, simply wouldn't do.

As we made our way home, I noticed my mother was driving towards the city. We didn't live in the city. "Where are we going?" I thought we might be going to see one of my aunts, or maybe even my grandmother to get my birthday money. She always gave me a dollar for every year, plus an extra for luck. I could do a lot with twelve dollars back then.

"I have to stop at the studio real quick."

I should've known that "real quick" didn't mean real quick. It never did with my mom. She was notorious for saying, "I'm just around the corner," before she had even left the house.

Apparently, the deadline for her submission was fast approaching. She used to submit her music to movies and television—I learned years later that this was called sync licensing. Time to record was already scarce, and the ad libs needed to be finished now so that it could be mixed and mastered in time. "It'll be real quick. Then we can get your day started, birthday girl."

I'll admit I was annoyed—this was supposed to be *my* day—but I wasn't too upset. I usually liked the studio. My mom had slowly started to purchase her own equipment, so that she could record at home whenever she wanted. She had taught me the basics, and by this time I knew how to record my own vocals and bounce it all to CD. The only thing she was missing was a professional microphone, but the lack didn't bother me. I would spend hours during the summer recording covers of my favorite singers. Back then, when you bought a single on a cassette tape, it would often include an instrumental. I had covers on top of covers—no idea where they ended up.

The real reason I liked this particular studio, however, was because of one thing: the PlayStation. I had my own gaming systems: my beloved Super Nintendo and a Nintendo 64, but the PlayStation was my favorite. I had one, but the games were pretty expensive, or at least according to my parents they were, so the only games I had were the ones on the demo disc. At the studio, though, there was an entire book of games. My mom would be upstairs recording, and I'd sit there for hours playing *Tekken* and *Crash Bandicoot*. There were other games I'd investigate, but those were my favorite. Sometimes, there would be other recording artists, rappers mostly, waiting for their sessions to begin, and they would teach me how to do combos. I liked them teaching me, but I liked it more when I was alone. Then I could play unbothered. That's how it was today. It was early on a Monday, and no one would be there.

Before we got to the studio, my mom stopped off at the gas station to get me snacks. She told the attendant it was my birthday, and he winked at me before sliding a lollipop underneath the glass divider and motioning, "Shhh." We hopped back into the car and were there before I finished unraveling the lollipop. The studio was in a house, and it was completely quiet. My mom mentioned once more that this would be quick, and I plopped down onto the couch with my black plastic bag and dumped my snacks onto it before turning on the television.

Before I knew it, the sun had started to go down, but this didn't alarm me too much. It was January, after all, and having a winter birthday meant the day would be shorter. The real fun was scheduled for tonight, so the sun setting only made me more excited. I remember getting up to go to the bathroom and looking into the mirror at the "new" me. I thought I looked older, more mature. I didn't fully understand the concept of maturity, but I knew that eleven was older than ten, so I obviously was one step closer to it.

Eventually I got bored of playing PlayStation games, so I went upstairs where all the recording took place. I knew how important it was not to ruin a take, so I waited until I could hear the music before entering. If I could hear it, that meant they were observing the playback, not recording, so I wouldn't get yelled at for ruining a perfectly good take.

I opened the door as soon as I could feel the bass in my feet. "Ma—" "I'm almost done!" she spat, before I could even finish. "Go sit down." I was tired of sitting down. I was tired of waiting, hell, I was tired in general at this point. I didn't say any of that, though; I just shifted slightly in the doorway before closing it to head back downstairs. I didn't turn the PlayStation back on, and for a while I didn't even turn the TV back on. I just sat there, daydreaming. Daydreaming all of the things I'd do once I finally got out of there. I'd narrowed my rental options down to three choices: *The Rage: Carrie 2*, *Halloween: H2o*, and *The Blair Witch Project*. My parents had seen the latter in theaters and hated it, so it was more for me; I was keeping the movies for five days, after all.

At some point I decided to turn the TV on, and that's when my night got even worse. The TV just happened to be on UPN and *Moesha* was on. This meant that it was 8:00 p.m. I was only allowed to be up for another hour. *The Parkers* followed, and we were still there. By the time *Girlfriends* came on I was pissed. Not only were we still there, but I hated *Girlfriends* (it's actually a great show; I would revisit it later in life). After being forced to sit there and let *Girlfriends* happen to me, I heard my mom coming down the stairs. I heard the engineer apologizing, and when I saw my mom, her face looked exactly how mine felt.

We walked out of the front door and down the salt-covered stairs to our car. She was silent until about ten minutes into the ride. "I'm sorry. The lead vocals were deleted, and I had to re-record everything." She did sound really sorry, and I wanted to say it was okay, but I didn't. It wasn't okay. Blockbuster was closed, my birthday dinner was cold, and *my* day had been spent doing what she wanted to do. I just sat silently looking out of the window and taking in the night view of the city. The city was always beautiful to me, but at night it was enchanting. I loved how nothing ever shut down. The streets were always filled with people, with adults, going about their business. I remember thinking that I couldn't wait to be an adult. When I was an adult, I wouldn't have to get trekked around, missing birthday dinners. I would be out in the city, with the lights and excitement. I had spent my entire birthday alone, so if I was going to be alone anyway, I might as well be alone as an adult with freedom. I couldn't wait to grow up.

Little did I know, growing up came in stages, and I was about to go through my first one. About a week after my birthday, my mom picked me up from school. She worked at her old (and my future) high school, Alan B. Shepard High School, as the speech coach. She was a fantastic coach, and her team was quite impressive. I remember being fascinated when I got to watch them practice. Today was one of those days.

The halls felt gigantic as I followed her past the walls littered with photos of my family members. They had all gone here, and the halls contained every class picture from the time the school had opened. I passed aunts, uncles, cousins, and people who were close enough to the family they might as well have been one of the three. We arrived at the practice room, and I set up camp on the tiny platform behind the teacher's desk. This way I could pretend I was doing homework but watch everything that happened.

One of the girls who went first was doing a monologue about having AIDS. I had only a vague understanding of AIDS (thank you, *Captain Planet*), but her monologue moved me. She talked about drug use, unprotected sex, and how her life span had been cut short. It really moved me. I wanted to go to the bathroom, but I didn't want to miss anything. I held it in until she had finished receiving her notes and correcting her performance before bolting out of the door.

I sat down in the stall, relieved, until I noticed something brown on my underwear. "What the—" I froze. I knew what this was, but I couldn't believe it was happening to *me*. We had learned about "our changing bodies" before winter break, and I knew that I was *menstruating*. But our book had said most girls experience their periods around sixteen, the earliest being fourteen—I was eleven! I went from being horrified to excited in a ten-second time span. I had heard the older girls talking about having periods. The *mature* girls. Does this mean I'm mature now? Have I arrived? I had heard about girls whose mothers took them to lunch to celebrate and have "the talk." I sat there for what felt like seconds thinking about where my mother would take me for *our* talk. I really liked IHOP, maybe we could go there? I loved that they had blueberry syrup, and our house only had regular old maple. Or maybe we could go to a buffet. I imagined us sitting at a round table for two, covered in a fancy white cloth, waters with lemon placed before us as I sat down with a plate full of chicken and dumplings.

In all of my daydreaming, I didn't notice my mother had come into the restroom. Apparently, I had been sitting there for a while. "Lori Tori, you okay?" I froze. What was I supposed to say? How do you announce this? *Yeah, I'm fine. Just some light vaginal bleeding because I'm mature now. No big thing.* Instead, I just opened the stall door so that she could see for herself. That seemed bright. "What's that on your underwear? Did you have an accident?" Why is that where her mind went? At eleven years old, her first thought was that I'd shit myself? I was mildly offended.

"No." I said and tried to get up. That's when it hit her.

"Hold on," she motioned for me to sit back down, and she tore some tissue from the giant roll sitting on top of the handy device it was supposed to be inside of. She fashioned a makeshift pad and placed it onto my underwear. She didn't say anything for a moment, then after I had finished adjusting myself and washed my hands, she said, "You got your period." I remember feeling extremely uncomfortable. Not from the tissue, although that was obviously annoying, but from the exchange. She didn't seem excited like I thought she would be. She seemed annoyed, like this was some huge mistake I had made, but I didn't know how to fix it. I felt ashamed.

Years later, I would learn that this was simply because this was not a momentous occasion worthy of celebration for my mother. Periods meant babies, and she had an older sister who got pregnant very young. We never discussed this, but I've always felt like that had something to do with her reaction. She wasn't mad, or annoyed that I had gotten my period so early. It was merely a harsh reminder of what awaited her daughter. I was young, innocent, and lived in my own little imaginary world. Menstruating only served as a reminder that this time wouldn't last forever, or even that long.

Years later, when I started studying theory, I would learn about Ferdinand de Saussure and how language is a sliding scale of signifiers and signifieds. For me, the word period meant a time of growth and excitement—one step closer to being the cool adult version of myself that existed when I closed my eyes at night. For her, it didn't have this same signified. A lot of the confusion and frustration I experienced as a child could have been avoided if I had discovered this sooner. I could've *told* my mom that *I* was excited. I could have *told* her that all of the girls on TV had celebrations when they got their periods and I wanted one too. I remember telling her once that all of my friends had seen *Spice World* and I *needed* to see it too. What did she do? She picked me up early from school, and sat through *Spice World* even though she didn't want to.

I assumed that my idea of what happens when a girl got a period was universal. It wasn't. I could have spoken up, but I didn't. I felt that familiar shift of discomfort, and instead I opted to keep the peace, or what I *thought* would keep the peace.

When we got home, I walked into the house quietly. I just wanted to disappear. There would be no celebration, no buffet, no talk. I went to my room and plopped down onto my bed. If this was what being mature meant, I wanted to send it back. I wanted to be a kid again; I wanted to not feel ashamed. Why did my period come so early? Was it me wishing to be an adult? Did I somehow bring this onto myself?

A few hours later, my dad came in, and I heard my mom tell him; it sounded like she was shouting. "Loreal got her period today?" I heard him ask. "Do I need to get some sanitary napkins?"

Sanitary. I felt dirty.

"We can get some tomorrow," I heard my mom answer. "She's not bleeding much, and I gave her some tissue."

The next morning, I woke up, and was relieved to discover I was no longer bleeding. Perhaps this was a false start? Perhaps I was still just a kid? I was excited. I ran to tell my mom the good news, but she was unmoved. "That's normal," she recited, "It'll take you time to get regular." Defeated, I walked back to my room and lounged until around noon. My dad came home from the grocery store and handed a bag to my mom. She thanked him and motioned for me to follow her into the bathroom. When I got in there, she motioned for me to sit on the edge of the bathtub, and she sat on the toilet.

"You've started your period. Do you know what this means?"

I shook my head no.

"It means that you can get pregnant now. Do you know how people get pregnant?"

Another head shake, no.

"Through sex."

I will spare you the details, but anyone who knows Sharon knows that she is blunt. I learned about penises and vaginas, and what happens when they introduce themselves to one another, but that this should only happen when you're in love and married. I also learned that sex is very painful for the woman because of Mr. Penis, and now I was fine with never falling in love or having kids—she described childbirth as well, and in a way that only Sharon can. Good times.

I walked away from that conversation more confused than I went into it, and despite her offering a Q&A section post story time, I didn't want to ask anything. I just wanted to get the hell out of there. Unfortunately, this sums up puberty for me: I was confused and just wanted to get the hell out of there. I seemed to do everything early. As the years crawled by, I was the first to have breasts, get acne, gain weight in interesting places, and by the time seventh grade rolled around I was already 5'6".

Despite my awkwardness, I managed to do okay in school socially. I was class president and had a core group of friends I'd known since second grade. Unfortunately, an incident with the priest (not in the way you're thinking) forced my parents to pull us from Catholic school mid-year, and I found myself at a public school with all new rules. Literally on day one, as I stood dutifully in the disorganized zigzag vaguely resembling a line, two girls rolled out of the abyss, engaged in a brawl over some guy. This was the first time I'd ever seen a fight like this up close, but it wouldn't be the last.

Junior high sucked. For the first time school wasn't my refuge, but a prison. My dad ended up getting a promotion, so we moved at the end of the school year, and I had to start over again. I wish I could say this experience was better, but it was actually worse. At least at my old school I had some neighborhood kids there to keep me company. Here I was brand spankin' new, and the novelty of being the new girl wore off real quick.

I hated eighth grade. It was a rough period—let's call it the lost year. I was smart, but being smart wasn't cool. I wanted to be cool. I wanted to date. I wanted to do all of the things that the other kids could do, but I couldn't. My scaries were really bad, and everything I did made me insecure. I had a habit of sitting with my legs crossed and overheard some girls making fun of that. I was "old-fashioned." I didn't wear hip huggers, and the thought of a thong made me uncomfortable.

I might have physically matured, but mentally I was far behind. I still liked Barbie and watched Nickelodeon while everyone else was rushing home to catch BET's *106 & Park*. I wanted to fit in, so some things had to change. Cue montage of me buying makeup, learning to shave, begging for microbraids, and changing my clothes after leaving home to the more form-fitting pants from Fashion Bug. I even bought a thong—despite no one ever seeing it, *I* knew it was underneath my hip huggers, and that was all that mattered.

Most of my eighth-grade peers would tell you that I fit in, that I was well-liked, that I was funny and a class clown. Inside, I was down bad. I felt ugly, lame, and like I was never enough. I have no explanation for feeling the way I did during this time, other than pressure—pressure I created. I wouldn't learn about "imposter syndrome" until years later, but that's the best way to describe this period. I was doing fine in every aspect of my life, but to me it was never enough. I was never smart enough, never pretty enough, never thin enough. I was hard on myself, and I don't know why. I tried so hard to be everything that everybody wanted, but I never stopped to ask myself what I wanted.

I wouldn't ask myself that question for another decade, at least, but ninth grade did get better. My parents were determined to get me back into private school, so off to Marion Catholic High School I went. I remember being petrified from day one. Years of *Boy Meets World* told me that I would get lost in the shuffle, and I came in fully prepared for that. Only, it didn't happen. Not only did I make friends, I started to discover myself. I even auditioned for the speech team, scaries and all.

I had prepared a comedy monologue. It was a scene that took place in the 1950s, the role was a busybody neighbor with a *Dennis the Menace* type son, and the entire monologue was the busybody trying to entertain guests while her son completely demolished the house. I put on my best 1950s housewife voice and really got into it. My classmates were in tears. My teacher was in tears. I knew I'd made the team.

About a week later, following rehearsals, the teacher held me back after dismissing everyone. "You're funny, but you already know that." I did know that. "I think you should try drama." He handed me a script from some play I'd never heard of. "If we only do what we're good at, we'll never know if we're better at something else. I think you'll surprise yourself with this one." I was hesitant—I hated drama. I just wanted to be funny. I took the script and waited out front for my mom to pick me up.

"How was school?" It was a question she asked every day, but today I actually had something of value to contribute. I sighed and explained what happened, telling her what Mr. Sweeney had suggested to me.

"Sweeney?!"

She repeated the name, as if she were asking an urgent question. Apparently, he had been a rival of hers back in the day—her response had suggested as much.

"You go back in there tomorrow and tell him you're a comedian. He's pushing this piece off on you because you're a freshman and no seniors or juniors want it."

"But we don't meet again for two weeks," I mumbled pathetically.

"Well tell him then!"

Only, I wouldn't get to tell him then. Over the summer, Keke had booked a role in *Barbershop 2: Back in Business*. It only shot for three days, but she was hooked. Unbeknownst to all of us, my mom had been communicating with people she knew in California. She'd been telling them that Keke was starring in the movie (she had one scene) and even sent them the audition tape that she'd used to prepare Keke for the role. There was interest from an agent in Encino, CA—he wanted to introduce her to the creator of *Moesha* and *The Proud Family*. So one extremely uneventful day after school, my mom made an announcement that would alter my life forever: "We're moving to California next week!"

3

Growing Pains

Life is often funny, in a way that only life can be. I remember being obsessed with the show *Full House* in the fourth grade. I loved the huge, two-story home they lived in, how the kids never received severe punishments for misbehaving, and how life just seemed to be generally problem-free for them— minus the whole no-mom thing. I mistakenly associated this way of life with California. Everything amazing in TV world seemed to happen in California. Almost every one of my favorite shows ended by telling me that it was filmed in front of a live studio audience in California.

After one particularly intriguing episode of *Sweet Valley High*—it was so much so that the only thing I remember about it is the theme song—I ran to my mom. She was sitting in her makeshift home studio trying to mix some vocals. "Mom, Mom, *Mom!*" I screamed as I tapped her shoulder. She removed her headphones, "What, baby, wha-at?" The last part came out a mix between singing and pleading. "Can we move to California?" She immediately turned her head and put her headphones back on. "One day," she said before resuming her music.

The following Monday I went to school and told all my friends that I was moving to California. Not one of them believed me. I remember being annoyed and embarrassed by their lack of belief. My mom said it, so it must be true. And it was—eventually.

That was the story I reminded myself of as I walked into school the Monday following my mom's declaration. *You always wanted to go to California, now you are.* The school had been informed I was moving, and the guidance counselor had summoned me to his office. I had been here a full quarter and never once interacted with this man. What was the point now?

I walked through the door to a room I never knew existed, in a part of the school that I never knew existed, and signed myself in. After a few minutes, an older gentleman, who I assumed was in his fifties, called me in to his office. (I've learned after having children that oftentimes kids' age estimates are off—my kids used to think I was eighty-five.) One thing that I'm certain of is that he was off-putting. He made me glad to leave the school. He was abrasive, and I remember being grossed out by how tight his pants were, and the fact that he decided to sit directly in front of me with his legs wide open.

"So why are you moving?"

Because my parents are making me. "My dad's job is transferring him."

No one told me to say this, I just felt like the alternative would require far too much explanation, explanation I did not want to give tight-pants man.

"Oh? What does your dad do?" He had a way of making everything feel accusatory, as if he was questioning whether or not I was really moving, or worse, whether or not I really had a dad.

"He's in sales."

This made him chuckle. "So, he can't sell here?"

This meeting was really starting to bug me. I had no idea what he wanted me to do. Jump up and shout, "You know what? You're right! I'm not moving, thank you for this guidance!" So, I just sat there, an entire class period, as he talked about the "horrendous state of California's politics." He trashed the state, individual cities, then went to town on the corruption of the entertainment industry. I wished I had told him the real reason I was moving.

When he was finished, he stood up, his tight-pantsed crotch directly in front of my face, prompting me to also stand. "Well, if you have to go, I wish you luck." He extended his hand, which I reluctantly shook while recalling the five thousand times he'd rubbed his nose during his rant. "Take care, Gloria."

Gloria? Who's Gloria? I nodded and left. Maybe moving wouldn't be so bad after all.

The week before the move crawled by. Everyone was excited but me. Other than the guidance counselor, I really liked my new school. In the sixth grade, a field trip to a local high school's production of *Guys and Dolls* had caused me to be bitten by the theater bug.

My mom and dad were both theater actors, and when I expressed interest in theater myself, my mom had told me, "Theater is fun, but you won't make money unless you're on Broadway." I thought I could be on Broadway. I was a big dreamer back then, but had no confidence that my dreams would ever come true. There would be no speech, I told myself, no *Taming of the Shrew*, no high school. Years later, I heard someone describe depression as the inability to imagine a future. I was definitely depressed.

A day or two out from our move, my cousin Denise invited me to a house party. We called Denise Lady Bug. Everyone in my family has these random nicknames. Sometimes I have to think really hard to recall their actual first names. This party was in the city, in one of our other cousin's, Buddha's, friend's basement. Normally, I wouldn't have even had the audacity to ask my parents to let me go to a basement party. This was different, though. We were moving, and I had been moping around for days. I deserved *something*. They apparently thought so too, because before I knew it, I was picking an outfit out of Denise's closet.

"Wear this one!" She threw me a red and white crop top, something I never would've been allowed to have in my house. We didn't wear the same sized pants, but luckily I had brought my favorite pair of Fashion Cents jeans. They were tight hip huggers made from different patches of denim. Lady Bug stole a belt from her older sister, one with a flashy buckle that said something like "hottie" or "cutie," for me to wear. The night before, Keke had given me individual braids, but she was only nine, so they weren't the most secure. I pulled them up into a high ponytail, securing them with a headband like I had seen Janet Jackson do in the film *Poetic Justice*.

You've heard of fashionably late? Well, we were ready unfashionably early. It's not like we had anything better to do. About an hour before the sun began to set, Lady's older sister

Natlie came home (not the one whose belt we had swiped). She noticed we were dressed up.

"Where y'all going?" She asked with a smirk.

I couldn't tell if she was genuinely curious or preparing some type of punchline for a lame joke. You know, the ones that older siblings use to make fun of the younger siblings, but the jokes are never even remotely funny? When I was at Lady Bug's house, by default, I, too, became a younger sibling. She was the baby of five, but she didn't act like it. In fact, I can recall many times when her older siblings would come to *her* for guidance.

"To a party," Lady answered. Her tone was short, and she didn't elaborate. I think that she, too, was unsure of where Natlie was going with this. Her smirk remained firm.

"Who's party?"

"Buddha friend," Lady answered.

Natlie's smile widened. "This y'all first high school party!"

Her intent was clear now. She hadn't wanted to embarrass us—not directly, anyway. She was excited now, asking who would be there (we didn't know), where the house was (we didn't know), how did Buddha know him (we didn't know). She seemed satisfied enough by our lack of answers and proceeded to give us advice. Natlie isn't too far off from Sharon in the bluntness department.

I will, again, spare you the details, but this time I learned that penis-havers lie to vagina-havers in order to facilitate introduction. But this time I learned that the introduction was not always painful, in fact, it could be downright exquisite, resulting in an explosive celebration at the end. I learned that one should only introduce themselves to Mr. Penis if he was wearing his gloves, because the getting pregnant and giving birth part was still horribly painful. What was *happening* at this party?

I had heard about city parties, but I'd never been to one. Three of my cousins attended Morgan Park High School on Chicago's South Side, and this was a party thrown by some random sophomore who had extended an invitation to any and everybody who'd heard about it. After it had gotten dark out, Lady Bug and I left her house to meet up with Buddha so that we could all walk to the party together.

"Woah, Loreal at a city party?" Buddha teased when we got to his house.

"Shut up!" We all laughed and went on our way.

You could feel the music coming from the party at the top of the block. Buddha stopped walking.

"Y'all stay together. It's finna be a lot of people in here. Somebody mess witchu, find me and my guys." He was older, though not by much, so I guess he wanted to create the illusion that he was our protector. He started walking again and we followed. "It's five dollars to get in, but y'all wit me." I'd never had to pay to get into a party before. I was starting to get nervous.

We reached the house and immediately I wanted to be back home. A "lot of people" had been an understatement. The crowd outside resembled what you would expect to see at a tailgate. There was music coming from the house and from the cars parked outside. The party had taken over the block, and no one seemed to care. People were dancing, shouting, chasing each other—it was a lot to take in.

Somehow, we made it in, avoiding the five-dollar entry fee, and made our way down to the basement. It was dark, except for a blue light bulb hanging from the ceiling in the center of the basement. The bass was intoxicating, and after a while I noticed how hot it had become. Lady Bug and I found a spot in the corner and observed the crowd. Occasionally, someone from school would recognize her, and they would chat for a while before moving on. I didn't know anyone, but I was oddly okay with that. I think the realization that I was leaving in a couple of days was somewhat liberating. Who cares if I did something to embarrass myself? It was highly unlikely that I would ever see any of these people again. I was free.

Eventually, we went from observing the crowd to being absorbed by it. We found ourselves in the center, dancing and rapping along to our favorite songs. A guy recognized my cousin and stopped to say hi. "What's up, Denise, you at a party?" It was always weird to me when people called her Denise. She had been Lady Bug our whole lives. She laughed. "Yeah, y'all got me to come outside tonight."

Lady Bug and I were very different. She was from the city, and I was from the suburbs, and it showed. She was more mature than I was and knew way more about dating and sex than I did. Even after my amazing talk with my mom. One thing we did share though, was the fact that we were loners. Neither of us partied much, or even stepped outside of our houses much—but for different reasons. I was afraid. She just didn't want to. She pointed in my direction, "This my cousin, Loreal." He looked in my direction and bit his lip. "What's up, Loreal?"

I smiled back, "What's up witchu?"

The rest of the night I talked to the boy. I learned that his name was Stacy, he was a sophomore, he lived up the street from Ada Park, and he was interested in me. We danced, and in case my mom is reading, it was lovely dancing where we stood six feet apart and never touched. After what felt like minutes, my older cousin found us and told us it was time to go; unlike them, *I* had a curfew.

We left the party and went back to Lady Bug's house. For a moment, I forgot I was moving. I forgot my life didn't matter. We stayed up talking about the guys we'd met at the party, and messing up her kitchen making pizza, wings, and cookies we'd never eat. At some point, we passed out, and when I woke up my dad was waiting for me. I said my goodbyes and got in the car. We would leave soon, and none of last night would matter. It was bittersweet.

At midnight, two sad days later, we left for California. Earlier in the day, I had kissed my grandmother goodbye, heartbroken by the thought that I wouldn't get to see her every day anymore. She crumpled money into my mom's hand when she thought the rest of us weren't looking and squeezed. "You can always come home, Sharon. Always." They hugged briefly, neither of them overly emotional, and my mom hopped back into the car. As we drove away from my grandmother's house, I was trying so hard not to cry that my throat began to ache. The tears fell after I could no longer hold them back. I turned my body unnaturally towards the window and stared out at nothing. I didn't want anyone to see me cry, not that I thought they would care. I remember being mad that my eyes had become so blurry; this was the last time I'd be here for a while, and I couldn't even see anything.

Now, we were standing outside of our home, with the family members who could make the trek at this awful hour to send us off. My uncle Dennis was a truck driver and had drawn the route to California on a map. His route would take longer, but it would avoid the dangerous mountains. My aunts and uncles hugged and kissed us, something they'd rarely done before. They were excited. None of them had ever left Robbins, other than the few who decided to live in the city, but even that was the extent of their travels. We were getting out, and whether it worked out or not, this was huge. Two of my aunts handed my mom some money. "This all I got," my Auntie Nene said. "Y'all get out there and do the damn thang." She smiled through tears and then turned her attention to us. "You going to Californ-I-A, Lori! Keke, you do that shit!" She hugged us tight, and we piled into the backseat of the car.

I was fourteen, Keke was ten, and the twins (Lawrence and Lawrencia) were two. I wish I remembered more about the drive to California, but I don't. I remember being bored out of my mind. These were the days before iPads and e-books. I had brought two Christopher Pike books with me, *Bury Me Deep*, and *Road to Nowhere*, which I finished before the end of the first day. The route we drove took us east before west, so the first night was spent in Arkansas. After dark, my dad pulled into the first hotel he saw. We got some fast food and piled into bed. I slept in one bed with Keke and Lawrencia, while my parents slept with Lawrence in the other. We woke before the sun and hit the road just as it showed its face.

An uneventful night was spent in Texas the next evening. We rose early again and were on the road. The next night my dad grew tired early, and we stopped at an Albuquerque motel before the sun even started to set. There was a grocery store next to it, so my dad walked over to buy snacks and rotisserie chicken. While he was away, my mom returned a call from Keke's agent.

Apparently, there was an audition the next day at 5:00 p.m. for an episode of the UPN sitcom *One on One*, and the agent really wanted her to make it. Even if we left now, getting to LA in time wasn't likely. My mom wanted to try anyway. When my dad got back, she expressed the importance of the audition. He was exhausted, and said, "She'll just have to miss this one," which frustrated my mom. "This is the whole reason we moved, Larry. We don't know if she'll even get any more auditions! She's not even officially signed to this agency! It doesn't look good to miss auditions." I could see where both were coming from. On the one hand, my dad had spent the better part of the day driving, and really just wanted to relax, finally. I don't think the audition was a high priority for him in this moment, understandably. However, my mother also had a point. Calls like this one *were* what we had started this entire journey for. If there was an opportunity, it should be taken. She knew very well how rarely they came along. Honestly, they both did. My dad was also an actor, and gave up a chance to go to UCLA and pursue acting in order to stay home and care for his mother. I think this is the real reason we found ourselves on the road to California: they both knew what it looked like to stay put, and they didn't want that for their daughter. Neither of their daughters, but I was too young to understand that.

My parents continued arguing over the best course of action, and I was annoyed. I made a comment, I can't recall exactly what I said, but knowing my mood, the fact that I was a teenager, and the fact that she was already irritated, I understood I had set her off, but I didn't care. The rest of the argument is a blur, but the gist of it was that she said something along the lines of being fed up with my bratty teenager vibe. I remember feeling all alone in the world—it was the worst thing that could've ever happened to me. But remember that concept I mentioned earlier, *tragic serenity*? I wish I had had some then, because in the grand scheme of things, this is a moment I think about as frequently as I think about the fact I used to like to take a magnifying glass to ants: not at all. This was probably the most exciting thing that had happened to me up until that point, and I spent it thinking no one cared about me. I felt insignificant and insecure, and no one had gone out of their way to make me feel like that. In fact, both of my parents would check in on me frequently, especially my dad—he, too, was a peacemaker, and he would try to let me pick out our food stops on the road, or pick a family game for us to play as we drove. What was my response? Let's just say if I had had an iPod, it would've been blasting Nirvana.

There was no *Full House* moment afterward where my dad sat me on the edge of my bed and assured me that I was loved and valued. In true Palmer fashion, when we were all done yelling, we just quietly ate and went to bed. The next morning was the same. There was no talking. We ate quickly and got back into the car. I don't remember anybody speaking the entire morning. We must have, though, because I can't imagine anyone in my family not talking for that long. Also in true Palmer fashion, we got over things quickly. By the afternoon, we were back to normal, well, as normal as we could be given the circumstances. I remember one of our favorite games to play was the "movie game." We would act out a scene from a movie that we'd all seen, and whoever guessed correctly had to pick the next movie. We were serious too! We would disguise our voices, play multiple characters, really anything to get as close as possible to the way the scene had actually played out. Movies were a big thing for our family (surprise, surprise), so this game could go on for quite a while. Usually until my dad would stop at a gas station to fill up and get snacks. Then we'd switch to the "song game."

The "song game" was kind of like the "movie game." We had to sing a section of a song, and the person who guessed correctly would get to pick the next song. Most of my family have beautiful singing voices, but my dad...well, bless his heart. He could take the most recognizable song known to man and have us all convinced we had never heard the song before in our lives; sorry to this man. I can hear my mom now, "Larry what are *you* singing?!" As we all laughed at how horribly off he was after he had revealed his song choice—sometimes the words wouldn't even be right.

As the sun started to go down, we crossed into California. For the first time since getting in the car, I didn't feel miserable. The palm trees looked so beautiful. I remember this strange feeling coming over me. Before we moved, my grandmother had told me, "You've always felt like a California girl to me. Hold your head up, pull your shoulders back. You've gotta act like you're from California now." Something *did* feel different as we entered the San Fernando Valley. I knew there wasn't anything *truly* different, but it felt like hope. Yes, we'd come here for my sister, but maybe good things were about to happen to me too.

I often joke that I've lived two separate lives. The old me died the night we left Chicago, the moment we hopped onto the expressway. Whoever that Loreal was meant to be, I'd never know. She never got a chance to grow. Maybe I was a phoenix, waiting to burn and rise from the ashes. Little did I know, I'd burn and rise many, many more times.

4

Family Ties

I won't bore you with every single little detail about our initial move to California—and trust me, it *would* bore you. Most of it consisted of trying to set up camp and figure out next steps. One really funny memory I have is of the first night we spent in California. My dad had to empty his entire retirement fund in order for us to make this move (this isn't the funny part). They wanted it to last, and we had no idea just *how* expensive California was, so my parents tried to stay in the cheapest motels possible.

I wish I could remember what this hotel was called, but the name (gratefully) escapes me. Anyway, we got all checked in, and were excited to finally be *there*—even dramatic me. I was smart enough to realize that staying in a hotel in the valley was super cool, especially as a former *Sweet Valley High* fan. We all packed into the double queen room and started to settle in. This would be our temporary home. It was a pretty standard hotel room, nothing special about it. It had two queen beds, a TV, an armoire, a nightstand, and some lamps—very ordinary. I remember just as we were all finally ready to come out of road trip mode and settle in, Keke jumped into the bed, got under the covers, and exclaimed, "Mom, my legs are itchy." I laughed, but my mom didn't hear her, because she was heading into the bathroom...which she promptly came out of, announcing colorfully that it was filthy.

My poor dad was so exhausted from the drive, he said something along the lines of leaving tomorrow, but that it would be good enough for tonight. Mom wasn't so sure, but she didn't press the issue...until my dad turned on the TV, where almost every channel we found was porn. That did it. My parents scooped us up immediately, and we drove around trying to find another hotel that wasn't as expensive as the one where Axel Foley stayed in *Beverly Hills Cop*. We will never know why her legs were itchy.

We found ourselves at the St. George Inn. It was a small, but cute, motel that we would call home for a while. We tried our best to create a sense of normalcy. I don't remember much of what was going on with the industry side of things, but every night we would have dinner together and watch *King of the Hill* and *The Simpsons*. I remember that for breakfast the motel would serve donuts, and Keke and I swore up and down that they were the best donuts we'd ever eaten.

One afternoon, while my parents went shopping for micro-wave dinners (we had no oven), Keke and I decided to play "shark" with the twins. It was a game we had made up (that I feel like every kid in America has also made up) where the twins would be in the bed, or the "boat," and we were the hungry sharks waiting to snatch their little legs into the ocean. This particular game of shark became intense, and one of the twins kicked as I tickled their feet. They hit me right in my glasses, which promptly broke. I was terrified of telling my parents. I knew that money was tight, and when you're blind as a bat, glasses cost a LOT of money.

I had micro-braids at the time, and strategically pulled a few from my ponytail to create a lengthy side bang in an effort to conceal the broken frames. I made it through dinner and was almost safely in bed before my dad noticed the frames leaning crooked on my face. As if he and my mom could communicate telepathically, I now found her facing me as well. "What happened to your glasses?" she asked, in that mom tone that warns you not to lie. As I told them what happened, I quickly followed with, "But it's fine! I can still see!" I didn't want them to spend money, so I convinced them that these frames were fine, but my parents refused to let me walk around with a missing handle, and my dad went to the local drug store the next day to purchase some reading glasses that matched my lenses. It worked...until it didn't.

You see, I have a nasty habit of sleeping in my glasses (I say *have* because I still do this) and this usually isn't a problem, but with these new frames that weren't made for my lenses, I woke up with the frames still on my face, but the lenses had escaped. My dad had to take me to the cheapest optometrist they could find, somewhere in Los Angeles, and this place was awful. The optometrist saw me quickly, but during my exam he kept falling asleep. I would start reading the letters out loud to him, and he'd go "mmhm, mmhm" then be silent. The first time, I thought I had mistaken his silence for sleep. By the fourth time, my dad and I were struggling not to laugh. Because my vision was so rough, I wouldn't be getting my glasses that day, or even the next one—there would be a two-week wait.

It's funny, I was in a new city, meeting new people, and having new experiences, but the mundane memories stick out to me most vividly. I remember spending hours online, reading message boards that dealt with girl issues like dating, periods, makeup, and how to have the perfect first kiss (not that I was kissing anyone any time soon) as well as boards that showcased original writing—fanfiction if you will. I stumbled upon a message board dedicated to creating stories based on WWE characters. I would get lost in the adventures of WWE Divas Lita and Trish Stratus for hours. I even wrote some fiction of my own, though I never shared it.

For a while, I was content. My dad had found a new job, and we would go to the company baseball games. I can't tell you if they were any good, but I *can* tell you that the nachos and hot dogs were amazing! Around that time we'd also moved into a small two-bedroom apartment. My parents gave us kids the master bedroom, and arranged it so that we'd all have some sense of personal space. We fell into a routine. Keke would have one twin (Rennie), and I would have the other (Thinker). We played school with them, pretending to teach them their colors and alphabet. I begged my dad to take me to Goodwill where I found old *Barney* and *Lamb Chop's Play-Along* VHS tapes—they had helped Keke and I learn, so I figured they'd help them too (although Keke was more of a *Big Comfy Couch* girl). We would dance to the songs, have nap time (Keke and I would work on homework), and when they woke up, we'd have graham crackers and apple juice. If Keke was out on an audition, I would tell them stories until my dad came home. Then we'd watch our beloved Disney Channel shows. Keke and I would get so invested in these shows, you'd think we actually knew the actors.

The days weren't all centered on the twins. Keke and I were homeschooled and had to complete our lessons. Because we weren't officially California residents (at this point in time, my parents had still thought this a temporary move), we were able to be homeschooled by Illinois standards. My mom had purchased books from some famous teacher store, and she would assign us homework. We were "supposed" to be doing our homework quietly for three hours a day. What would actually happen is we would goof off and listen to *Maury* or *Jerry Springer* from the dining room table. My dad started making us turn the TV off, but we would just turn it down really low, and when we heard their bedroom door open, we'd hit the off button on the remote. We were pretty quick.

But on one occasion we were not quick enough. This particular day, we were really rambunctious. My dad had to tell us several times that he would "break us up." It was an empty threat—where would he send us? So we waited for him to walk back to his room and close the door. Thinking we were in the clear, we resumed our activities talking (loudly) about the *Degrassi* episode "Shout." We must've gone on for twenty minutes, when we hear my dad say, "I've been watching you guys for a long time, and I don't see any school happening. Keep talking, and see what happens." Then as quietly as he had entered, he disappeared—and we erupted into laughter.

A little less than a month after arriving in California, Keke booked a national commercial for a Target ad. This was her first commercial audition, and friends of my parents who had gone to California before had told her that commercials were the bread and butter of actors who weren't "superstars", so we celebrated that night, with pizza. My mom and dad would often talk at night when they thought I couldn't hear, and they were both worried about me, due to my only socialization being with my younger siblings. Looking back, I can absolutely understand their worry. I've always been an extremely introverted individual, possessing an over-active imagination. Following the move, it was very easy for me to fall into my own imaginary world. The less I was around people, the less I needed them—I think this is where my imagination as well as my ability to keep things in really started to grow; I was slowly becoming self-contained. Mom told Dad she wanted to start including me more in the entertainment business process. The first audition I went on with Keke was for a small role in an episode of a new crime drama called *Cold Case*. The episode was titled, "The Letter," and it was about a 1930s brothel where one of the women had been murdered. Keke's character was the daughter of the woman who ran the "boarding house." She was the only person who could read or write, so she would write letters for one of the Black women who had been engaged in a love affair with the white milkman. It was an intense storyline, to say the least.

Keke ended up getting the role, which would shoot for about a week, but I wasn't allowed on set. A work holiday gave my dad an off day, so Mom told him to take Keke to set so that she could take me and the twins shopping. Although the show filmed for a week, she wouldn't be needed for the full week, so he took an additional day off to accompany her. I was told to pick one inexpensive outfit, and the twins would get a toy each. My dad had our only car, and he was at set with Keke, so this meant that we would take the bus. We were used to taking the bus in Chicago with no problems, but here, taking the bus was quite the adventure. Somehow we got turned around, and my mom's phone died. She was getting frustrated, and I didn't know how to help. A lady overheard her thinking out loud and offered to let us use her phone at home. With very few options, my mom agreed. It was a single lady with a newborn infant. Seemed harmless.

Her apartment was an extremely small studio. She apologized for the size, but we didn't care. We just needed to use the phone. My mom called my dad's cell, and he mentioned that they were just wrapping up, so he could come get us. We gave him the address, and sat with the lady to talk while we waited. She proceeded to tell us her entire life story, which was *wild*, and then started mentioning how lonely she was. I felt lonely a lot as a teenager in a new place, missing my friends and my cousins, so I decided to engaged with her. She then asked me about myself, while occasionally licking her lips in a suggestive way as I responded. Needless to say, Sharon stood up and said, "He should be here soon," and started to make her way toward the door. The lady asked me to come back and visit her again anytime, saying, "You can even come by yourself." I did not.

As we left, my mom explained to me the importance of reading the room. I wasn't picking up on the woman's advances. This was an important lesson for me to learn out here in this new world and I'm thankful that my mother was there with me. Although I doubt that this woman would've tried to get rough with me, we were in a new city, a new industry. We were not in Robbins, IL and we had to move accordingly. This isn't to say that there were no men or women waiting to take advantage of me back in Robbins, but what this does say is that we were no longer in the familiar and we had to be aware of our surroundings at all times; this was a lesson for maneuvering both in life and in the entertainment industry—to this day I am always reading the room, reading people. People rarely do things without motivation.

My days off set weren't always that eventful. Usually, I'd stay home with the twins while my dad worked and Mom and Keke were on set. I didn't know how to cook much, so I'd repeat meals a lot. I mostly cooked breakfast items, which they loved: pancakes, eggs, oatmeal, grits, and toast. Occasionally I'd grill cheese with bacon. Meat scared me. I knew it could all go south real fast if it was undercooked. My favorite time of day was always dinner. My dad is an amazing cook. I have friends to this day who will ask, "When is your dad in town? I need some of his greens!" Even if he was just making hot dogs and French fries, it would be the best hot dogs and fries I'd ever tasted. I would ask him to make me sloppy joe all the time, because his sloppy joe was way better than the sloppy joe at school—and the school sloppy joe was good! My all-time favorite though will always be the pork chops. When I would ask him what was for dinner, he'd turn to me doing his best Peter Brady impression (he knew I loved the *Brady Bunch*) and say, "Pork chops. Pork chooops and applesauce." Back home, dinner was an isolated affair. We'd make our plates and go back to our rooms and eat as we watched our own individual shows, but here, it was a group activity. One of our favorite shows to watch with dinner was *Law & Order: Special Victims Unit*.

After Keke finished filming *Cold Case*, things quieted down for a while. Pilot season had ended, and the holidays were approaching, which meant we were all home together more often. Our apartment was across the street from a Rite Aid, and when our parents had a little extra money, they would let us walk there to buy whatever we were into at the time.

When we weren't doing schoolwork (or slacking off), we'd watch movies. I had been telling Keke about *Candyman*, and how it scared me so much at seven years old. She begged us to watch it one night, and after convincing my parents that she was old enough at ten, they let us rent it. We watched it during the day, because I thought it would make things less scary for her—it didn't. She was afraid to go to the bathroom by herself for a good week. I'd hear her running to and from the bathroom, leaving the door open as she went.

A huge audition for Keke came up around Christmas. It was for a movie with William H. Macy called *The Wool Cap*. My mom went into speech teacher mode. She made us all sit around the table and do a table read of the script, minus the twins of course. Then she asked us questions about Keke's character, Lou. What was her motivation? What inspired her attachment to William H. Macy's character? Did we know anyone in our real life similar to Lou that Keke could use for inspiration? Questions none of us had the patience to consider or answer.

Mom was a professional amongst novices. My dad at least tried to play along, but these table reads would go on for what felt like hours. If that wasn't bad enough, they were always followed by her filming Keke, and I had to stand off camera and feed her lines when what I really wanted to do was curl up in my bed with a good book and the Disney Channel playing in the background. She would do this over and over and *over* again. At the time, I hated the "rehearsals," but later I would get it. You see, she wasn't just working with Keke, she was working with *me* too. All of her techniques would show themselves in me years later, when writing an essay, creating a presentation, or competing on a reality show.

Keke ultimately received a callback, which meant the process with my mom would repeat. For weeks, we lived, breathed, ate, and slept this script. Then Christmas came, literally and figuratively, and we found out she had gotten the part. They were filming in Montreal, and we couldn't all go—TNT (the network producing the film) would only pay for Keke and one parent. I was excited for Keke—she had worked hard to land this part. But I was sad that I wouldn't get to go to Canada, home of *Degrassi*!

But it turned out that I would be offered something much better. One morning, while I was lounging on the couch, my mom walked into the living room and sat down next to me. "How would you feel if you and the twins went back to Chicago and stayed with Grandma while Keke and I go film this movie?" I sat up. "Where would Dad go?"

"He would stay here in LA and work. It's a three-month shoot, so you would stay with Grandma and go to the local high school until the end of the school year. Then we would all come back. What do you think?" That was all I needed to hear. I jumped up and down screaming, "Yes! Yes! Yes!"

My mom smiled. She seemed relieved.

We didn't have long to get ready, maybe a week at most. I packed all of my stuff, said my goodbyes to Mom and Keke, and then my dad drove us to the airport. The plan was for him to fly to Chicago with me and the twins, help us get settled for a couple of days, and then fly back for work on Monday. This was my first plane ride, and I remember being terrified when we were about to take off. Before I knew it, we were in the air. The plane was pretty empty, so my dad sat in the middle row with the twins and let me have the window seat row to all myself. I was in paradise, happily munching on my snacks and reading another Christopher Pike book, *Final Friends*, that I had just picked up. I loved the supernatural horror genre (I'd later learn this was actually cosmic horror) and devoured every one of his books back in those days. Secretly, I had wanted to be a writer. I had this vision of living in a house on a lake, with a huge office that had lots of windows so that I could look out of it and be inspired by nature. After I discovered Stephen King, I imagined this house being in Maine and on a cliff overlooking the ocean. I wanted a balcony so that when the weather was nice, I could sit outside and just write for hours. I wanted the house to be old, maybe Victorian, with lots of rooms filled with bookshelves. My wants were conflicting, because while I imagined my house being old and filled with forgotten furniture, my office had to be modern. I guess I didn't really know what I wanted, other than to write horror, mostly anthologies, in an old house overlooking some vast body of water.

I was almost finished with my book when it was announced that we would be landing soon. The twins and my dad were passed out. I thought about waking them up but decided against it. Instead, I looked out the window and watched as we descended into Chicago. This city that had enchanted me so as a child hadn't lost its touch. I could only see pinpoints of light from at that altitude, but I knew the people were down there, awake and on the move. I imagined where they were going—to parties, friends' houses, maybe even dinner and a movie. Wherever they were going, they were home here in Chicago. They didn't have the looming time deadline that I did.

I'd only been in California a couple of months, but the cold stabbed right through my thin jacket the moment we stepped off the plane onto the jetway. Had it always been this cold in Chicago? My uncle Reggie was waiting for us as we came down the escalator to baggage claim. "Hey hey!" He flagged us down, swooping us all into one giant hug. My dad's side of the family are the huggers. It was late, and I was tired. I must've dozed off in my uncle's car on the drive from O'Hare, because I only remember getting to my Grandma Palmer's house and passing out on her couch. We would spend one night there, since she was closer to the airport.

I had gotten used to California, but I missed my home, and my extended family. In California, everything seemed to revolve around the entertainment industry, with everyone playing a role to get ahead. But here, those roles didn't exist. Here, I would get to just be me. I would be the main character in my own story. I would get the opportunity to become the girl I started becoming before I left.

5

Family Matters

I woke up in the morning and someone had opened the blinds in the living room of my Grandma Palmer's house. I remember looking out and being so excited to see snow on the ground. We had left Chicago in October, just before snow would've started to fall, and despite the below-freezing temperatures that came with it, I realized I missed winter snowfalls. My dad and uncles made breakfast, and then my dad took me shopping to get new school clothes.

I was excited to be home, excited to be staying with my grandma, though less excited about her lack of cable television. This meant I wouldn't have access to my usual lineup of shows, so I begged my dad to take me to my favorite thrift store, St. Vincent De Paul, that always had the best selection of used books. I left with two full bags, loaded with every Christopher Pike book they had that I hadn't already read, some R. L. Stine *Fear Street* novels I hadn't heard of, and a few other books that looked like they had potential.

By the time we got to my grandmother's house, it was getting late and my dad had to head to the airport, so he picked us up some dinner. He gave us all hugs and kisses and asked us to behave, which was obviously a formality considering the twins were two and I would never dream of misbehaving—not at grandma's house at least. As I watched my dad walk out the front door, I felt tears beginning to form. I was happy to be home, at least I *thought* I was, but this wasn't exactly the way I wanted to be back.

I fell into a routine of waking up and eating breakfast, reading until lunch, then reading until dinner, then writing in my diary before reading until exhaustion. This lasted for a week or two, until school started. My grandma stayed home with the twins, and my aunt took me to the local high school. It was the same high school she had gone to, and that my mom and all of her siblings had gone to. It wasn't my old high school that hosted overnight lock-ins and movie nights, but I had been desperately craving the socialization of a normal high school experience, and there were other teenagers here so it would have to do.

And though I wasn't exactly popular at my new school, I had friends. Despite my grandmother being old-fashioned, I actually had a life and lots of freedom. I took the bus to and from school, and I was even allowed to go out with my friends after I had "gotten my lesson," which was how my grandmother referred to doing homework. Some weekends I'd even get to go spend the night at Lady Bug's, and we'd catch the bus to the mall, or to the library so that we could go online. Most people have heard of MySpace; we were on a similar site called Tagged. It worked the same way, and we'd spend a lot of time searching for cute boys to "tag." Sometimes we'd even talk to them. I wasn't allowed to date, but that didn't stop me from flirting, and it didn't stop boys from coming 'round to my grandmother's house looking for me.

I stopped thinking about my parents and Keke. My mom and dad called every night, and my mom would tell me about what was happening on set. Usually the updates were mundane and routine: today she filmed two scenes, we just came back from dinner, today she only had one big scene. Often, she sounded worried and tired. Once she called while I was asleep to let my grandma know that she had been rushed to the ER. When I woke up, my grandmother had led me to believe (somewhat dramatically) that something was wrong with my mom's heart. I found out later it was more like a combination of indigestion and anxiety—a prelude to future issues I'd experience myself.

About a month into my Chicago return, I woke up to someone squeezing and kissing my face. I opened my eyes, and it took me a moment to realize that the face I was staring at was my mom's. She was smiling the widest I'd ever seen, and she didn't even wait for me to fully wake up before she started squeezing me and crying. She was so happy to see me, and I was happy to see her too, eventually—once, y'know, I woke up. She decided to give my grandmother a break for the weekend, so she took me, Keke, and the twins to stay at a hotel. We checked in and then went out to eat. Then she told me that she had saved up some of her *per diem* and wanted to use it to buy me new clothes for school. We went to all of my favorite stores, and I literally got a completely new wardrobe. Tons of sneakers (gym shoes as we called them), handbags, and she even took me to get a second hole in my ear after Keke and I had gotten our nails done professionally. The weekend flew by, and just as quickly as my mom had appeared, she and Keke were gone again.

While I was in my room reading one night, I overheard my grandmother on the phone with my mom. She had been gone for about three weeks now. My grandmother was trying to whisper, "She had a gentleman caller, Sharon. I'm too old for this. Old folks don't belong raising nobody. My nerves too bad." She called me to the phone to talk to my mom shortly after, who was all too eager to gush about my "gentleman caller." I didn't even really like the boy who had come over, and the one guy I *did* like I was too chicken to do anything about. He lived down the street, and I had changed my bus route to ride with him. We were friends, but I never learned to move past that. I still don't know how to move past that—I'm perpetually friend-zoned.

Life in Chicago continued along. I went to school in the mornings, came home and read in the evenings, and on the weekends my grandma and I would begin our horror extravaganza. My grandmother loved horror movies as much as I did, and every Saturday around noon, the UPN network would show some B horror movie, usually from the '80s. My grandma and I would laugh our asses off as we ate popcorn and Jell-O (I wasn't allowed to eat any other snacks because I was getting "hippy"). Then, at midnight, we'd watch the horror hour on channel 26. The host, Svengoolie, played classic horror movies and then did sketches and told corny jokes before and after commercial breaks. I loved Svengoolie; he had long black curly hair, and wore a top hat, with heavy black eye makeup— picture a zombie Slash. My grandmother would lie in her bed, wrapped in her nightgown, stocking cap covering her rollers, teeth safely removed and placed into her brown coffee cup. I'd lie on the floor in an oversized T-shirt and socks, hair wrapped in a silk scarf, afraid to move when they showed a particularly scary movie—usually anything about religion or voodoo did the trick.

I would only have this one semester of high school, and it was a damn good one. Having been pulled from school allowed me to see just how much it mattered to me. I'd always been excited for high school, but behind the excitement, I still felt held back by my fear and anxiety. This time, I really immersed myself in my environment. I wasn't as shy, I got involved (albeit in a very limited way due to having to come home and help with the twins), but my hope had been renewed. I remember taking the end-of-the-year tests, and our teachers stressed how these years would prepare us for college. I started to imagine college. I could see myself there, but I knew my time in Chicago was coming to an end, and if I went back to California, I felt like I'd never have a life. I'd never have a future if I went back to California—my life was *here*. I just proved that. I wouldn't exist in California, not fully. There was nothing for *me* there.

The week before I was supposed to fly back to LA, I begged my mom to let me stay in Chicago. "Please, Mom, please let me come back for sophomore year, please!"

"Won't you miss us?"

"No! I'll see y'all all summer, and for Christmas and stuff."

"I can't be away from my babies."

"They can go with y'all. I can stay with grandma. She likes me here."

I knew when she said her "babies" she meant all of us, not just the twins, but I didn't want to go back to California.

Especially if it just meant more homeschooling. And it was true about my grandmother. She and I had always been close, but living with her these past few months had only made that bond even stronger.

One evening after school, I was sitting at the kitchen table eating dinner, and my grandmother just watched me quietly. She didn't take her eyes off me, and it was starting to make me uncomfortable. When I finished eating, I got up to go wash my plate.

"I found your book," she said.

I dried my plate off and placed it back in the rack. "Which book?"

"The one with your writing."

Fuck. She had found my journal.

"Oh." I said as I sat back down.

"You're a good writer, Loreal, especially your poetry. I didn't know you were so sad, though." She smiled, but it was a pained smile. She thought I was unhappy being there with her, but I wasn't. I was probably the happiest I'd been in a while. But I had written a sad (depressing, it was depressing) poem about hope and how I no longer had any.

I didn't want her to think I was unhappy there, so I stopped reading and writing so much, and spent more time with my grandma. We watched TV, went to thrift stores, I even got her to go to Blockbuster a few times to rent horror movies. There were so many she hadn't seen, and I loved watching her scream, "Run! Run! He's coming, you better run!" The one time we watched a tame movie, *The Lizzie McGuire Movie*, it bothered her more than Freddy Krueger ever could. In the beginning, Lizzie had ruined her eighth-grade graduation by tripping over the curtain and bringing the whole setup down onto her classmates. "Why'd you show me this picture? I hate that this happened to her." She fell asleep before Lizzie even made it to Rome.

My grandma became a surrogate mother, maybe even a best friend, and as much as I didn't want to leave school, I didn't want to leave her more. "Please, Mom! What if I get straight As?"

"You think you got straight As?"

I knew I didn't get straight As. I'd be lucky if my report card had even *one* A.

"Maybe," she paused, thinking about it. "If you get straight As, we'll talk." She told me she loved me, and we hung up. Maybe I could lie? She wasn't here, and this was before the days of fancy smartphones prompting proof. I could beat my grandma to the mailbox, and just lie.

I did not beat my grandma to the mailbox, and despite her promise that she wouldn't tell my mom, she did. And, just like that, I was booked on a flight back to California that weekend. My dad couldn't come this time, so my cousin Whitney flew back with me, to help with the twins. She would stay for a few weeks before going home.

Have you ever hated something so much that your brain refuses to form any memory of it? That happened here. I don't remember packing. I don't remember going to the airport; I don't remember even being on the plane. The next thing I remember is swimming in the pool at our apartment with Whitney the day before she left to go back to Chicago and being painfully jealous that I wasn't going with her.

I was back in California. Keke was fresh off of a movie. Things were picking up, and my parents were finding it hard to manage Keke's career and a household, so they came to the conclusion that for now it made sense for my dad to quit his job. This way, they could alternate between traveling to auditions with Keke, and being at home to keep the house running effectively. Word in kid Hollywood was that whoever the actress in *The Wool Cap* was would get busy. Even though I was in a house full of people, I felt alone. I was fifteen, the twins were three, and Keke was ten. Coming off of my high school high, I wanted nothing to do with any of them, and yet I couldn't escape. I remember being snotty, then feeling guilty, so I'd go back to peacemaking and do whatever they wanted.

My mom had a friend from Chicago who had moved to Los Angeles years ago, Leroy. He'd gotten a job working with a guy named Ralph Farquhar. Ralph had written on *Happy Days, Fame, Married...with Children, Moesha, The Parkers*, and my favorite, *The Proud Family*. Her friend had arranged a meeting. There was no project, just a meeting to "see where things went."

My mom hated the family being split up during *The Wool Cap*, so now she was dead set on us all going everywhere together, all the time. So, she made us go meet Ralph too. She piled us all into our white 2001 Dodge Caravan, and my dad drove us into the Hollywood Hills. I remember thinking we were going to fall off the edge. The way those roads twisted and turned, there was no way we *weren't* going to fall off the edge.

Somehow, we arrived in one piece at the largest house I'd ever seen. I was terrified as we walked up to the front door. How was I supposed to act? How would the twins act? They were extremely rambunctious by this point, and my mom and dad would be schmoozing, Keke would be "auditioning," and I would be left to guard Chucky and the Leprechaun.

The minute we got into the house, the twins went wild. Ralph had a mini pond in his living room. And there were actual fish in it. Lawrence tried to dive in after one of them. I was mortified, but the adults laughed. I wanted to listen, to take part in the conversation, but every so often my mom shot me a look that said, *please make sure the twins aren't demolishing this man's house*, so I spent the entire meeting making sure they didn't break an item that would cost more than a whole year's rent at our apartment. I was relieved when it was time to leave.

Not long after the meeting, Ralph called my mom. He'd written a pilot, and he wanted to pitch it to Disney. He sent the script over, and my mom made us do the whole table-read routine. The script was actually really cool, and I allowed myself to get excited. Even though I was warned that pilots didn't always turn into shows.

My mom gave me the news that I would get to go with her and Keke to the Disney meeting. Pulling up to the Disney building in Burbank was surreal. I remember walking in and feeling such awe. It looked like a regular office building, but this was where some of my favorite shows and movies had been created. I legitimately felt inspired. I remember thinking that if I could be here now, I could surely be here again, with something that *I* had created. I fancied myself a writer, after my many fanfiction series, and I went into the meeting hoping to leave an impression. I don't know what kind of impression I thought I'd make, but I wanted to make some kind of statement. I was talented too (as a writer, I could never act), and maybe I could show that; maybe if my opinions were asked, I could express that. I had zero idea of how a pitch meeting worked.

A friendly Disney Channel executive personally gave us a tour of where the magic happened. He showed us the DCOM vault, paying special attention to the ones they no longer aired. At the end of the tour, we sat in a large meeting room, waiting for the president to show up. When he finally came in, my mom and Keke went to work. They had a routine: my mom would mention how Keke sang in our church, then she would tell Keke to sing, Keke would playfully decline, my mom would prompt again, then Keke would act bashful before bursting into "Be A Lion" from the film *The Wiz*. It was entertaining to watch. The Disney executives were visually impressed. They were even more impressed with her knowledge of the channel. I left the meeting without leaving an impression, there wasn't really any opportunity to, but only one word can accurately describe how I felt leaving that building: sublime.

Not long after, we got a call that Disney wanted to shoot the pilot with Keke. My parents were so excited. Keke was so excited. I tried not to get my hopes up too high, remembering that Keke's agents had said pilots don't always work out, but I couldn't help but get caught up in the excitement too.

6

Three's Company

As we began the audition process for the Disney Channel pilot, *Keke & Jamal*, I started to feel *in the way*. No matter how much my mom made every effort to include me, I felt more and more displaced. I would go with them to all the meetings, table reads, and wardrobe fittings, but while my mom and Keke were expected to be there, I was like this bonus item that they weren't sure they wanted. In all honesty, it was just my teenaged insecurities. Without a reason to be there, I felt like I shouldn't be. Years later, I ran into someone from that time who shared that they always found me hilarious. Isn't it funny how our minds can play tricks on us?

Once the pilot was fully cast, it was time to film. This, I had been told, was the exciting part—and, in many ways, it truly was. Andre Jamal Kinney (*NYPD Blue*, *Hannah Montana*) was cast as Keke's older brother, Jamal, and Vanessa Hudgens (*High School Musical*) was cast as her nemesis. Both Hudgens and Kinney had been acting since early childhood, and both would go on to be cast in major hits for the Disney Channel. They were both older than Keke—my age, in fact. Being on set and hanging out with them provided a much-needed taste of socialization, but there was an ever-present reminder any time they were pulled for hair and makeup, or run throughs: they were actors and I was not (Not that I wanted to be. My mom and dad tried with me first, but it was not my thing—I was too afraid). But being on this set, where they had a purpose, was a stark reminder that I had yet to find mine.

Unfortunately, my skin wasn't thick enough then to understand that it wasn't personal. No one on set went out of their way to treat me differently, but I wasn't part of the cast, and I felt this.

It takes roughly a week to shoot one episode of television. Sitcoms only truly have about two days if they're filmed in front of a live studio audience. For this pilot, film days were Thursday and Friday. Monday through Wednesday were spent rehearsing the shit out of everything so that shoot days went as seamlessly as possible.

This moment was genuinely surreal for our family. I don't say this lightly. Never in our wildest dreams did we imagine Keke would book anything on this level. It was truly a humbling experience. My parents invited family from Chicago to attend the live taping. Even in my depressed "woe is me" state I understood the enormity of the moment, and I was excited to hear that my dad's brother Reggie could make it.

Uncle Reggie was one of our favorite uncles. Most people who met him felt the same way. He was naturally charismatic, and even when he was talking nonsense, you couldn't help but listen. He didn't really work, unless you count the polls during election years, but I always thought he'd make a hell of a salesman. Even my maternal grandmother, Mildred, who didn't like many people, loved Reggie. "How's your uncle with the loud mouth?" she would always ask. "He tickles me." He was one of those people who knew everything and nothing at the same time.

He arrived late on a Tuesday evening and rolled through the door of our new four-bedroom home in Altadena, still wearing a huge winter coat and scarf, which looked silly in the balmy October California weather. That's right, between *The Wool* Cap and the pilot, we purchased a house. My parents finally realized that California wasn't a pit stop—we were Californians now! People were in awe of how fast Larry and Sharon were moving, but knowing my parents, I wasn't.

After hugging and kissing us all, he called me over to the couch where he was sitting. "I got something special for you, Lori," he said solemnly. Birth-order hierarchy was important to my dad's side of the family. No matter what any of my siblings accomplished, my status would always be higher because I was the oldest.

He reached into his coat pocket and pulled out a paperback. "I know you like the scary stuff. Have you read this?" I took the paperback into my hands. The cover was wrinkled and chipped at the corners, like he had purchased this book years ago when he was my age. The title on the cover read: *Night Shift*, by Stephen King. This was the master of horror responsible for some of my favorite movies, but I had never actually read any of his short stories or novels. I was so excited you would have thought my uncle had just handed me the keys to a brand-new Porsche.

"Thank you!" I squealed. Uncle Reggie smiled. "There's some really scary ones in there too." I didn't waste time.

Immediately, I went to my bedroom down the hall (I had my *own* room now) and started devouring every story in the collection. I don't think I slept that night.

I don't remember much of the Thursday shoot, which was for pre-taped scenes, but the electricity of the live shoot on Friday was like a jolt of adrenaline. Everyone on set knew just how much was riding on the success of the pilot, but for my family, it was simply one giant thrilling experience. We didn't dwell much on the fact that the audience was a test, or that focus groups would be instrumental in the final say of whether *Keke & Jamal* would become an actual Disney series or not. We were in the moment. The crowd ate up the jokes. With each take, Keke transformed her delivery based on what elements of her last performance the audience had responded to most. I remember thinking that she was a natural—simply born for this. How fortunate she was to discover her calling at such a young age. Most of us aren't that lucky.

We were warned that it would be a while before we heard anything, but "a while" is relative. Uncle Reggie went back to Chicago, Keke went back to auditions, my mom went back to managing, and I went back to...well, nothing—unless you count reading. I had finished *Night Shift* in one sitting and was on the hunt for more Stephen King. By this point, we'd enrolled in a legitimately recognized California homeschooling program, and when I was really bored, I'd find myself knocking out a month's homework for a course in a weekend. I took as many literature classes as I could, growing particularly fond of British literature. There was something enchanting about Chaucer's *The Canterbury Tales* that made me think I would be content with studying the work and British lit in general for the rest of my life.

College was around the corner for me, and although my mom saw a future for me in entertainment as well, (I was a writer, I loved telling a good story whether it be prose, poetry, or a song. She truly believed in my ability to write music and films) I felt the classroom calling my name. My dad believed in my abilities as well, and would encourage me to write and sing, but he was also beginning the college conversation. It was partly because of him and the stories he would tell us about his college days that I really wanted to go to a university and live in a dorm. We heard about how his twin brother flubbed the registration forms, so Dad had to room with a stranger, and when he walked into his room, the first thing he saw was a rubber chicken, and a prosthetic leg. We grew up around his frat brothers who felt like actual blood uncles (we were honestly shocked to learn they weren't as kids). College was a life-changing experience for him, and I knew I'd need it to end up where I thought I wanted to go.

I wanted to teach ninth-grade English. My own freshman year English teacher, back in Chicago, had been amazing. She was a small, bubbly woman who loved to read, and hoped to get our class to love reading as well. She realized I hadn't needed to be won over, and that was that. I hated the books we read in her class, but I loved our class discussions post-reading. Her personality was so infectious that even those who didn't do the readings ended up joining in.

I wasn't having those discussions now. I didn't even have a teacher—not in the traditional sense. For one hour twice a week, Keke and I would go to a learning center in Irwindale to meet with a "teacher" who was primarily there to proctor exams or sign off on course substitutions. He wasn't interested in literature or lively discussions, so I usually just took the tests and waited the time out while reading. Keke interacted with him more than I did—she hated tests and welcomed all distractions. She was hilarious, and the other students taking exams during our time slot loved her being there; it meant nothing would get done.

Sometime during our waiting to hear about the Disney pilot, Keke booked a lead role in the Ted Danson film *Knights of the South Bronx*. Based on a true story, the screenplay was about a group of inner-city kids who learn to compete in chess. It was being filmed in Toronto, and this time my mom was intent on bringing me with them, while my dad stayed home with the twins. Keke was a lead character, so my mom was able to negotiate that I be allowed to come too since she was homeschooling me as well. She even let me have the other first-class ticket with Keke while she took a coach seat, because we had never flown first class before.

My only other experience on a plane had been the two flights I had taken from LA to Chicago and back, and neither had been this extravagant. The flight attendant brought us warm cookies and milk, which I'm sure she was only supposed to do once but did multiple times thanks to Keke's gift for persuasion. That five-and-a half-hour flight was the closest we had been in a while. We spent the whole time goofing off and trying to scare each other with our most terrifying made-up stories, all of which turned out to be hilarious due to our over-explaining the gruesome details of the monsters that had seemed so scary inside our heads:

"His eyes were so big," one of us would start, and then the other would jump in, "that they fell out of his head and started rolling around on the ground. Then they grew legs." When it just made no more sense, we found ourselves in hysterics. The ridiculousness was infectious, and I noticed people in the row behind us chuckling at our silly game.

When we arrived in Toronto, we had to fill out these international visitor cards, and that's when it really hit me—I was traveling outside of the country. Yeah, it wasn't Europe or somewhere drastically different, but I was *traveling* somewhere new; something extremely cool was actually *happening*. We exchanged our per diem at the airport, and Keke and I were enamored with the colorful Canadian currency. We were here to film a movie, but you wouldn't know it. We were two little girls from Robbins, IL, staying in a five-star hotel in Toronto—in a whole different country!

The front desk of the Grand Hotel in downtown Toronto knew we were there to film a movie (most of the other cast had already arrived as they were coming from New York) and were extra kind, telling us about all the sights the immediate area had to offer—the CN Tower, Eaton Centre, a science museum, and there was a ferry we could take to an amusement park.

Our room wasn't fancy by most standards, but we were impressed. It wasn't the Hampton Inn we had stayed in as kids for family staycations, and it surely wasn't the cheap motels we called home when we first moved to California—to us, it was a palace. We jumped on our beds (well, Keke jumped, I just kind of plopped onto it) and took our shoes off before asking our mom what was next. She was tired, I could tell, but she didn't want to make us stay in the room. There was a welcome dinner the next day, so tonight we could swim!

We didn't have much to compare it to at the time, but this pool would still be impressive after all the fancy hotels I've now stayed in. It was the length of a basketball court, the water was crystal clear, with navy blue stripes running across the bottom. We weren't the first kids there. In fact, most of the other four child actors cast in the movie were already down there swimming, while their tired, jet-lagged parents sat on the sidelines, watching them burn off energy.

One of the kids was a well-known child actor named Malcolm David Kelley. By the age of fourteen, he already had an impressive list of credits under his belt, including lead roles in the critically acclaimed *Antwone Fisher* and the community acclaimed *You Got Served*. But he was probably best known for playing Walt on ABC's hit show *Lost*. He and Keke hit it off from the start. The other kids were mostly new to the industry. They were all much younger than me, but I was used to being the oldest and instinctively slipped into the big sister role.

A few of the parents were my mom's age, but the rest were in their early to mid-twenties, and a lot closer to my age—in my mind I was a mature sixteen-year-old, so after a while I got out of the pool and started chatting with them. One of the moms, Sonya, was Dominican. She spoke very little English, but interestingly I got along with her the best. The English she did know was from TV and music, which happened to be the same shows I watched and music I listened to.

The interactions in Toronto made me feel like I had an actual, normal, teenage life. I'd hang out with the younger moms on set while the kids were filming, then during downtime I'd hang out with the kids. One shoot in particular was filmed at a local school that had been shut down. We had been warned to stay off the third floor, which was deemed unsafe. Naturally, we had to check it out. There were other kids there as well, working background, and the few we hit it off with decided to explore that floor with us. It was dark and dusty, so of course we were in heaven.

The floor looked like an abandoned parking structure that had been converted into a cafeteria that had then also been abandoned. In the center, there were what appeared to be about five large tables. Well, what I assumed were tables because they were covered in large, heavy, burgundy-colored plastic tarps. Everything was coated in a thick layer of dust, and one tall, lanky boy decided to run his finger across the tarp to spell his name. Scattered around the room were piles of unidentifiable junk that stretched almost to the ceiling.

There were no cellphone flashlights back then, so our only illumination came from the sliver of sunlight piercing through a missing plank from a boarded-up window near the ceiling. I felt a thrill of excitement. I wanted to find *something*. We all did. We fanned out and started poking around the floor, until...something decided to poke back. Suddenly, we all saw something scurrying in the shadows at the far corner of the room. It was either a demonic clown or a mouse. We will never know because all of us ran screaming back to the stairwell. We were running and shrieking so loudly, we ruined the take on the next floor.

Production was frustrated with our antics, but my mom was furious with *me*. I was the oldest and should have known better. I wasn't too bothered, though. I was a kid being a kid. This was what kids did. Sue me.

They did sue me—kidding! It was forgotten before the day's work had ended.

The six-week shoot went by faster than I wanted it to. During that last week, everyone was talking excitedly about returning home, about getting back to their lives, back to their loved ones and friends. But I had nothing to go back to. Yeah, the twins and my dad were there, but I could see them anytime. I wasn't ready to go back to being stuck in the house all day. I wasn't ready to return to a life that didn't involve actual living.

But it happened. I got on the plane despite my mind screaming at me to turn around and run all the way back to the Grand Hotel. Never mind me not having a room, or even money to get one. I got on the plane, and mourned Toronto the entire flight back to Los Angeles. Years later, I would reflect on Toronto fondly. In California I didn't really have an *active life*—I didn't belong to anything; I wasn't doing anything *for* me; I was waiting for things to happen *to* me, completely unprompted. In Toronto I felt like I did belong. I felt like I had a purpose, I had a routine, I had a reason to get up every morning, and I think that's what I missed the most.

LA was just as I had left it—yay. I resumed my monotonous existence, focused on school more than ever. I wanted to finish...I *needed* to finish. A quintessential high school experience was out of the question, but I *could* have a college one. I could go to a university, live on campus, maybe even join a sorority despite my inclination towards antisocial behavior. I felt like college would finally be *my* time. I wanted to follow my dad's dream.

With more money available these days now that mom and Keke were regularly working, I became a frequent shopper at Borders bookstore (RIP). I was a rewards member and everything. During one trip, I forced myself to walk past the fiction section, and on to the SAT prep workbooks. I wanted to go to UCLA. It was my dad's dream school, and since I couldn't go to his actual alma mater (Northern Illinois University) due to now living out of state and wanting in-state tuition, I decided this would be the next best thing.

I studied night and day, and even bought a book of Edgar Allan Poe's collected stories and poems that was supposedly littered with SAT words—it was a tremendous help that I absolutely loved Poe. My grades were great...except in math. I've always hated math, or rather it hated me, so I found myself stressed over my rapidly tanking grade point average (GPA) due to Algebra 2—the devil's language. I decided to take a page from Keke's playbook: the Art of Persuasion.

At our next weekly, one-hour check-in at the homeschool center, I decided to talk to the teacher. I tried to channel Keke's gift of charm. I started with some random talking point to encourage further conversation. It worked. Once I had him hooked, I segued into my math struggles, rambling on about my GPA, and blah blah blah.

"I just don't know what I'm going to do!" I lamented, with what I hoped was just the right amount of despair, "I'm not getting this at all!"

He was a nice man, very sympathetic to my tremendous plight.

"Would you be interested in taking Personal Finance instead?" he offered.

What? No!

"Oh, absolutely! That would be so much easier to follow!"

It wouldn't be. Not for me.

He smiled, pleased with his solution, happy he could offer me an alternative. After officiating the switch in the system, he went to the back and grabbed my brand-spanking-new Personal Finance textbook. The accompanying homework packets were retrieved from a large black and silver filing cabinet located in the center of the office. He handed them to me, just in time for me to notice my dad arriving to pick me up. I smiled, thanking him again. And made my way back to the car—no other homework would be finished until I completed all ten packets for this damn class.

Focusing on getting into UCLA gave me a renewed sense of purpose. I didn't just want to get into a good school, I wanted a new *life*, and UCLA was my window of opportunity. I barely left my room much during this time. I'd make an appearance to make a plate of food and bring it back into my room, or sit in the living room to catch an episode of VH1's *Flavor of Love* with Keke (which Dad hated). My books were always there with me, waiting for me to open them during a commercial break. I was in work mode, something heavy.

About a month after I had received my new Personal Finance course, Keke booked the biggest role of her career thus far—biggest to *us*. It was for NBC's *Law & Order: Special Victims Unit*. When she got the call, we all went crazy. If we ever had a family show, this was *it*. We all loved Olivia Benson and Elliot Stabler, so this was the opportunity to end all opportunities—we would *all* be going to this shoot.

We still hadn't heard anything about the *Keke & Jamal* pilot, but we didn't care. We were going to see Olivia, Elliot, Captain Cragen, and the gang. Nothing else mattered. The only thing I remember about the flight to New York City was the descent. Keke and I had a fancy new video iPod and a Gameboy Advance now, so we didn't talk much. Only to tell each other what was going on in each of our video games.

Landing at JFK Airport at night reminded me of arriving in Chicago almost a year earlier. The city was so vibrant, so alive. Even from thirty thousand feet, I could sense its life force.

There was no doubt in my mind that everybody walking those city streets below me did so with purpose—they had places to go, things to do. There was also no doubt in my mind that *soon* I would be one of those people.

Unfortunately, like "a while," *soon* was relative.

7

Working Title

We didn't get to our hotel until well after midnight. The only thing open near us at that hour was a pizza joint down the street, so my dad walked over to pick up a couple of pepperoni and sausage pizzas while the rest of us settled in. The hotel was like something out of a movie. It wasn't particularly fancy, but it had an old-world charm to it. It used to be an old apartment building that was converted to a hotel. In fact, one of the "guests" was a resident that couldn't be removed despite the renovation. Apparently, her unit was untouched since the '90s, but the building had been standing since the '60s, so I heard. I was hoping to catch a glimpse of it as she opened the door, to see what the building had once been, but I never did.

I remember falling in love with New York, but I can't exactly say why. My best guess would have to be that it was the same situation as Toronto—I fell in love with the sense of being out in the world with a purpose; it was a rarity these days. No, we weren't there for me, but I had things to do. It wouldn't be just sitting inside the house ruminating on my pathetic existence.

Most of Keke's scenes were shot on location around the city. This set was different from any we had been on. This wasn't the chaotic energy of a sitcom, or the sense of routine that resulted from a film set. This wasn't *our* set. We were guests, and they made sure we felt welcome. Unlike a typical sitcom, every day was utilized for filming, but Keke wasn't needed every day. The days she wasn't on set no longer reside in my memory, but the days that she was remain crystal clear.

Her first scene was before her character met Elliot and Olivia. It took place in a park, so I found a nice picnic table underneath the shade of a nearby tree and worked on my Personal Finance coursework. Something about the environment inspired me to be productive. There was another girl on set. She was a bit younger than Keke, perhaps eight years old, and the two hit it off well. She had the energy of both Lawrence and Lawrencia wrapped into one. She was sweet, but my patience ran out quickly. She had a million questions that would always lead to a million more questions. She had a new trick every twenty minutes that she just *had* to show you, and she spoke so fast it was a mental workout just to keep up. In other words, she was a typical eight-year-old, but I was a typical teenager and I didn't really want to be bothered. Her grandmother was a sweet woman, and I liked being around her. She made me think of my own grandmothers back in Chicago.

Set days were long, eight and a half to nine hours, plus travel time. Leaving was always an event. Once Keke was wrapped, she had to change out of her set clothes—and getting a twelve-year-old to change was always an event. Then she had to sign out. Child labor laws are strict—child actors are *not* allowed to stay on set even a minute beyond the point that the legal maximum hours had been reached. Sometimes when Keke had been extra energetic, I could feel the stress heat emanating from the sweaty first assistant director as he waited patiently outside of her trailer for her to emerge and sign the timesheet.

What little energy any of us had left as we were rushed into a car that would take us back to the hotel was gone by the time we made it back. I don't remember eating or turning on the TV—just getting into bed and entering the deepest of sleeps. During those days, I was more comfortable in a hotel bed than I was in my own back in Los Angeles. Sleeping away from home, away from the suffocating monotony of my own life, was always more peaceful. It was an escape.

Keke's first day on set with Elliot and Olivia (a.k.a. Chris Meloni and Mariska Hargitay) was surreal. I was completely starstruck. Chris Meloni made a point of introducing himself when he saw my mom and me sitting in the corner, trying to make ourselves scarce. He asked us questions about ourselves, and I could barely summon the courage to respond—did I mention I was a huge fan? If he noticed, he didn't hint at it. It was all so natural as it unfolded, but truly sublime at the same time.

Mariska Hargitay came next. Literally one of the sweetest women I've ever met. When she shook my hand, she squeezed it tight and told me I had a beautiful smile. To this day, I still tell people this story. Mariska Hargitay thinks I have a beautiful smile! I don't care what anyone ever says about me or my looks, I know my smile is solid! For a teenage girl who never thought of the word *beautiful* in association with herself, this was a huge boost to my self-esteem. She said other things too, but I can't remember. I was too busy smiling.

The rest of that set experience is a blur. Keke's final day of filming took place at the police station. I wish I had taken photos, or even written in a diary, anything to look back at now and remember more. I can't even remember the flight home, or getting home, but obviously it happened. I was back to studying, back to sitting in my room, back to having no life—at least, that's how my dramatic sixteen-year-old self viewed things. I hated not being physically in school, but I had grown to love traveling. Honestly, looking back, I was just extremely confused. I craved the teenage life I grew up watching on TV, from Cory Matthews getting his first kiss, to DJ Tanner stopping Kimmy Gibbler from drinking at a party, heck, I even wanted to work on the beach for a summer job like Zack Morris and the gang. But by now I'd realized that what I *was* getting was also special. It was something that most people will never experience, and part of me was starting to enjoy that—I just didn't see my place in it. Not in an attainable way. I couldn't travel with Keke forever, she would grow up and so would I, then what?

At some point we found out that *Keke & Jamal* hadn't been picked up. Instead, Disney had decided to pick up a little show called *Hannah Montana*. I think in the end it worked out for all involved. They were very clear, however, about wanting to keep a relationship with Keke, and hopefully work together very *soon*. The auditions resumed, and we didn't really mourn the loss like we thought we would. It was a part of the business. A part that we all had to learn to accept.

We didn't know it then, but a big audition was on the horizon for an independent film called *Akeelah and the Bee*. I won't bore you with the details, as we all know how this audition ends. To this day, people still refer to Keke as "little Akeelah," which is pretty amazing when you stop and think about it. It would be ten years before I actually watched the movie for the first time. The impact that film had on people was really special, but it was something I couldn't see back then. I knew that she was amazing in the role, and I knew that this was *huge* for her, but I was young, and I lacked the ability to see just how huge it really was. When I finally did watch it, I cried like a baby. The pride I felt watching her play little Akeelah was indescribable. She wasn't my sister on that screen, I *felt* her performance. It's one of my favorite performances of hers to date.

I was excited that Keke got the role, but I was devastated that it was going to be filmed in Los Angeles. There would be no travel, no escaping my actual life to inhabit a cool new fantasy one. Instead, I would go to the set on some sound-stage or studio lot downtown and then return home at the end of the day to my own room in my own house. The best thing to come out of this set (for me anyway) was Jo Ann Smith—Keke's studio teacher, who as far as I'm concerned is the best there ever was. She was a kindred spirit to us both. Miss Jo Ann was all of my favorite childhood teachers rolled into one. She had a way of making learning fun, and she even let me do my schoolwork with Keke in the bungalow assigned as the on-set schoolroom.

Child actors are legally required to spend three of their eight to nine hours per day on set (depending upon age) in school. Keke was in almost every scene of *Akeelah and the Bee*, but she could only be on set filming for a maximum of six hours. This was a low-budget film, so they needed to be completed in about thirty days—they were attempting the impossible. A workaround was that Keke could bank hours on a day that she wasn't scheduled to work. When they had to pack a lot of scenes into a day, they could pull from those banked hours and now have her for close to a full workday.

Keke and I lived for bank days. Miss Jo Ann was an avid reader, and she would meet us every Saturday at our favorite spot, the Borders in Pasadena, with a new list of books for us to check out. We'd sit at the bookstore's coffee shop, Seattle's Best, and do our schoolwork as she read and tried to keep Keke from getting too distracted. Keke was the master distractor, but Miss Jo Ann always knew just how to get her back on track in a way where Keke would know she had been defeated—though only temporarily. Miss Jo Ann started learning which way each of our own personal tastes leaned and had little lists of things she thought we might like to check out. She would make deals with Keke: if she completed a certain amount of work, she could take ten to fifteen minutes to read the book she had bought for her. In a way, I feel like Keke clung to these moments just as much as I did. She had to exist in a grown-up world for most hours in the day, but here, with me and Miss Jo Ann, she got to be a kid.

One book Miss Jo Ann brought was about a group of kids who had died and were stuck in the afterlife running from some monsters. Keke wasn't a reader, I was, and she often had a lot to read with all of the scripts, auditions, and schoolwork, but Miss Jo Ann sold the book to us. She would tell just enough to have Keke on the edge of her seat before saying, "We can read the next chapter after you finish these few math pages."

Keke wouldn't even huff or puff. She'd just pull out the math book and get started.

"How many do I have to do?"

"I'll set a timer, and when it goes off, you can either read it or I'll read you some more."

I don't think she really set the timer. Just when Keke was starting to get visibly antsy, she'd say, "Okay, Keke. Would you like to read now?"

She had great film recommendations as well, and her set stories were always a good time; so was her humor—still is, I love seeing her Facebook posts.

The *Akeelah and the Bee* set was great, but the real action started after filming wrapped. Mama Sharon had heard that the soundtrack for the film was in need of some original music, and she was making moves. Keke could sing and I could write, so in her mind this meant we *belonged* on this soundtrack—it was the perfect way for Keke to segue into music, and for me to break into songwriting. I wasn't against the idea, but I wasn't necessarily for it either. I liked to be invisible. By this time, I'd gotten really used to blending in. Standing out was scary.

Music was something that came naturally to the women in our family (although my dad will tell you our musical gifts come from him, bless his heart). As a young girl I'd wake up to Grandma Mildred singing gospel music on Sunday mornings. It was the only time I heard her sing, and she had the voice of an angel. Like my mother, it was one of those powerful, soulful voices that you just knew had experienced some things. I asked her once who my mom had gotten her singing ability from (before I had heard her sing), and she said my grandad. He used to sit in the back room he had built onto their three-bedroom home and sing loudly to blues records.

Songwriting was a skill that came directly from my mother. I had grown up learning to record my own music before I had fully mastered cursive. Those same instrumentals that I had used to record endless covers of my favorite artists—Mariah Carey, Britney Spears, and Eden's Crush—had also been utilized to accompany my own lyrics. I spent full afternoons, and sometimes evenings, in my mother's home studio writing and recording songs like the ones I had heard on the radio. *My man left me, my man cheated, I have a new man now, I'm in love with two men*—things I knew absolutely nothing about. At some point, the songs transitioned into things I *did* know about: *I've been crushed by my crush, why won't he notice me, why does love have to hurt*—good old dramatic teen music. Eventually, I would become angsty and write punk music, but we aren't there yet.

My mother had some old friends who had come to California years ago in order to "make it" in the music business. They were record producers who had endless tracks, but no one to add lyrics. That's where we came in. Mom had put the word out amongst her circle that the *Akeelah and the Bee* soundtrack was looking for music. Daily, we'd have new stacks of tracks to comb through. My mom booked studio time, and we'd all brainstorm lyrics based on the vibe of the track. I probably felt most alive (outside of when I was traveling) during these studio sessions. I had a purpose, and it was something I was *good* at. Something I knew and had passion for.

At some point, we received news through a friend of my mom's that Atlantic Records was interested in signing Keke. My mom arranged a private screening of *Akeelah and the Bee* for the company execs and a host of well-known music producers and writers at a theater located at the Lionsgate headquarters. By the end of the night, the reaction of the bigwigs had solidified that life was about to change for us.

Shortly after that, we started receiving more tracks. Some contained a verse and a chorus, others just a chorus. The word was still out there that Keke, by which my mom meant both of us, *had* to write on the record. One recording session proved very fruitful. We were working in Will Smith's recording studio, The Boom Boom Room (which would later become like a second home), with a team of writers known as Tha Movement. They had verses and a bridge down, but we needed a hook. To many, the hook is the most important part of the song—the part that gets stuck your head and pulls all of the other elements together.

We sat there forever, trying to find something catchy and meaningful, since it *was* for the soundtrack of an inspirational flick. I sat in the corner of the room, humming a melody quietly to myself as I typed the lyrics on my laptop. My mom overheard me and asked, "What's that? What are you singing?" I was nervous, because it wasn't ready yet, but I sang what I had, and to my surprise, everyone liked it. Satisfied with the hook I had created, she got into the booth, recorded the vocals, and the session ended. Tomorrow we would present what we had to the VP of Atlantic Records.

I wasn't nervous. Well, I wasn't *too* nervous because I knew I wouldn't have to perform. But the lyrics to the hook *were* mine, and I had this horrible thought in the back of my mind that the VP would hear what we had come up with and say, "Everything is good but the hook. It sounds amateur. Who the fuck wrote this?"

He was friendly when he came into the room shortly after we had finished our lunch; personable, and great at small talk. Finally, it was time to play the song for him. The producer hit play, and he listened with a stoic expression planted onto his face. Occasionally he would nod.

Outside of one small comment regarding some preposition changes, he liked it. He *really* liked it. I had just written on my first professional song, at sixteen. I could technically call myself a professional songwriter, which definitely made the dream seem more attainable. Now we just had to get the guy in charge of the soundtrack to like it. I remember feeling so proud of myself. For a moment, I had forgotten about Personal Finance. I had forgotten about school, period. My mom was also very proud of me. She couldn't contain herself. "Loreal, do you realize that this could lead to a publishing deal? You are really talented!" The hook of "All My Girlz" holds a special place in my heart.

From that point on, we spent more time in the studio than we did at home. My room that had once been both my sanctuary and my prison had now become a place to lay my head. Most of the early sessions would take place at The Boom Boom Room, but occasionally a writer based in Los Angeles would prefer us to come to his studio. One of those writers was a guy named Mischke who would share stories about working with Michael Jackson, and tons of other artists like Tupac Shakur, that would turn our eyes into saucers. Sessions with Mischke were some of my most fond memories from this time because he seemed to genuinely want to write with us.

One day, we asked him what his last name was. With a name like Mischke, we just knew his last name was just as cool.

"It's a boring last name."

"What is it?" Keke asked.

He smirked, "I'm not telling you."

She begged periodically throughout the session, but he never told us. Later that night, we Googled him extensively and finally found his last name. Once we had it, Keke messaged him. His response had us in tears from laughing:

"Wow! I'm impressed! I've never been Googled by a celebrity. This is hilarious...almost as hilarious as the fact that you two have been to my house a million times with all of my magazine subscriptions with my full name plastered across the cover."

We couldn't wait until our next session with Mischke. Very few writers seemed to view us as anything more than two kids whose mom they wanted to appease, but Mischke was always teaching us.

Another one of the few was Toby Gad. He'd written Fergie's "Big Girls Don't Cry," one of my favorite songs. I was honored to work with him, but not honored enough. During this time, I had become restless. I had been to what felt like hundreds of writing sessions, and of those a good 75 percent had obviously started before we had gotten there, because within minutes of our arrival a completed song would appear, and all Keke would have to do was sing.

Why am I even here?

Songwriting had become a burden. I felt pressured to write something, anything, but if the collaborators don't want to collaborate with *you*, what can you do? Nothing. So that's what I did. I started to retreat. I'd bring my Personal Finance textbook that I had started to ignore to sessions with me, and I'd pretend I was writing on my laptop every time my mom came in to check on how things were going. I wish I hadn't done that. Toby Gad was like Mischke—he cared. The lessons he taught me about creating a story through music are some I still use to this day in all my writing. For example, start with the title. The title prepares the listener (or the reader) for what they'll be listening to. Then from there, ask questions of the title. With "Skin Deep" I think one of my questions was: What is an example of looks being skin deep? From Mischke I learned melody, and improving harmonization.

Atlantic Records sent us to Atlanta to write with an extremely talented group of songwriters known collectively as The Clutch. They wrote "Ice Box" for Omarion and "Like A Boy" for Ciara. Two of my favorite songs. We also wrote with singer/songwriter The Dream, who had been responsible for Rihanna's "Umbrella." During these sessions I didn't even bother trying to write. Not only had I lost my zest for writing, I had also lost my confidence. These were heavy hitters with songs actively in rotation on the radio. How could I possibly keep up? What did a seventeen-year-old know about writing a hit record? I didn't want to write hits. Music had been fun for me, therapeutic. I quickly realized that I didn't want a career in music. I loved it, but not hard enough.

I struggled through Personal Finance in Atlanta, and by the time we landed back in California, all I needed to do was turn the work in. I was officially a high school graduate, a whole semester early. I still wanted to go to UCLA, but there was a problem with my homeschooling program that stopped me from going straight into a UC (for those unfamiliar with the two public higher education systems in California: UC, or University of California, and CSU, or California State University). UCLA was my dream. I could've gone to a CSU, but that's not what I wanted.

I was tired of not getting what I wanted.

While finishing up Keke's debut album, *So Uncool*, I enrolled at Pasadena City College. I juggled classes and studio sessions, being partial to the classes; the sessions felt more like a job. My new sanctuary became English 1A. It was a class that took place off-campus, at La Cañada high school. I was one of three PCC students in a room full of high school students—it was a dream come true. It was a surreal environment for someone who was pulled from high school after a partial freshman year. I was in my element.

One night, there was a recording session that took place during my English class. We needed to finish the album. My mom and I argued for hours as I told her I wasn't missing class.

"This is an opportunity," she said, calm but deadly.

"But I have class," I whined.

"School will still be there, this opportunity will not," she said solemnly. "You have to make a choice."

I had tried her way. It was time to try mine, but my brain wouldn't allow me to commit to it. I wanted to say no, to attend my lecture, but I didn't. I didn't really know how to. School was important to me, or least really starting to become important, but this was the family business. I've always had a problem with trusting my own instincts, plus part of me was still pretty insecure about school despite loving it; missing a formal education still made me insecure, even though I was excelling. What if it didn't work out? What if I bombed my other classes? I was slowly beginning to develop this warped view that the entertainment industry was more reliable than any other career because Keke had been successful. What I had yet to realize was that Keke was so successful because she genuinely loved what she was doing. Even if she had zero fans, she would be happy performing. I liked writing music, and I liked writing scripts, but when I saw myself in the future, I didn't see myself exclusively doing either one of those things. But it was easier to take the path of least resistance, and in this family it appeared, to me, at that time to be film. I missed my favorite class to write the song "Bottoms Up."

8

The Real World

The album was finished and had a release date of September 18, 2007. I was about a month into my first semester of college. The studio sessions had ceased, and life had moved on. That first semester kept me sane. I once again felt like I had a purpose, but it was different this time. Every other time had felt like a dream I would wake up from, but this? I felt like I could spend the rest of my life in school and be legitimately satisfied.

I ended the semester okay—I was rusty and earned my first (but not last) B in English. The other courses were fine, a C in sociology, but I'll admit it was 100 percent on me (I hadn't done a lot of the work). I have this horrible habit of going all-in obsessively with the things I love while ignoring the rest. That was definitely what happened here. I was in my element in English. I liked writing, even academic papers. My classmates were so impressed with my writing voice, and during workshops, peer reviews always left me feeling both embarrassed and proud. This was something I was good at, but I had to work for it. Music seemed to come naturally, but I had to work to write a good paper. Nothing compares to the feeling of finishing a paper you're proud of and adding that Works Cited page. I lived for my professor's feedback so that I could make the necessary corrections. I couldn't wait for my second semester.

But wait I would. I registered for Spring 2008, but I didn't attend. In December of 2007, shortly after my last day of classes, Keke booked a role for a film that would end up being called *The Longshots*. It was the true story of a little girl who played on a Pop Warner football team, in a small town not too far from the one we had grown up in. The film starred Ice Cube and was directed by Fred Durst, which was very interesting to me at the time, since I had been a Limp Bizkit fan.

My mom asked me if I would like to go for a bit, before the semester started. I really missed traveling, so I said why not? Every new city left its mark on me, and the people I'd meet did as well. I didn't know this phrase at the time, but each new city, new experience, new encounter was allowing me to "fuse my horizon of understanding." Every lesson or word of wisdom shared on the road would turn up later in life. While the experiences were enlightening, they were also plenty. Mom would give us an allowance from the per diem, which we'd use to go shopping and eat at fancy restaurants. For me, it was like getting paid to go on vacation. The movie was filming in Minden, Louisiana. I had never been anywhere in Louisiana, but I'd heard the food was good, so I was game.

We had to take two planes, one from Los Angeles to Dallas, then a small plane from Dallas to Shreveport. Our LA flight was delayed, and by the time we made it to Dallas, they were preparing to close the gate for the flight to Shreveport. We raced through that damn airport barefoot with our shoes in our hands. We got there just in time...for them to say sorry. The next flight wasn't till tomorrow night, as it was a small airport that didn't receive much traffic.

That simply wouldn't do for my mom. She was getting us on that plane.

"Please, my daughter is the star of a movie," she started. "Filming starts tomorrow, and we can't miss this flight. It could cost millions!"

Catching on, Keke and I looked pitifully at the guy manning the gate. We had his attention.

"Which one of you is in the movie?" he asked.

"Me," Keke shot an innocent smile.

"Where y'all coming from?" he spoke as if we had more time than we actually did.

"Chicago. We're just regular people," was the response my mom gave.

Maybe he was just regular people too, because the next thing I knew he was saying something into his walkie-talkie and we were being let onto the plane. There were two rows of single seats separated by an aisle. We all sat by ourselves, Mom on one side, Keke in front of me on the other. Out of ten, maybe fifteen seats, there were only three other passengers in the very back. I had never been on a plane that small. Keke passed out before we had even taken off. She had a gift for sleeping on planes back then. Simply fastening her seatbelt would flip some invisible switch, and she'd be out like a light.

It was only a forty-five-minute flight, and sleeping seemed pointless to me, so I pulled out a book and read. I was deep into Stephen King and currently devouring *The Tommyknockers*. I had really wanted to read *Needful Things*, but I couldn't find it anywhere, and someone had checked it out at our campus library and never returned it. It would be over ten years before I started it—I'm still not finished.

We spent three months on the set of this film in Louisiana. It was not supposed to go this long, and I was too young (plus I didn't care) to know what exactly went on behind the scenes. What I do know is that I had the time of my life. It was a set full of kids, and it felt like summer camp. Keke's stand-in (someone on set who looks like the actor/actress and literally stands in for them while the crew sets up the cameras and lights) was a girl my age, and we were the counselors. She reminded me of my cousin Denise, and we both melted into a friendship quite easily. She was funny and very outgoing. She made me feel at home in this town that was new to me. She invited me to events all the time, but my mom wouldn't let me go.

"I don't know anybody here. Somebody could kidnap you and then what?"

"Moooom! I'm too big to get kidnapped!"

"They kidnap grown folks too," she'd reply, sounding like Mildred.

I remember this set and the *Jump In!* set (filmed in Toronto) fondly for so many reasons, but the main one being the social life they provided.

Even at PCC I would just go to class and come home. I didn't really make friends easily. Leaving high school had stunted me in that avenue. I missed three years of socializing with my peers, and by the time I enrolled in community college, I felt awkward. What if I didn't remember how to talk to my peers? Everyone I communicated with then was either way younger or way older. Did I know what was "in"? What was hip and cool (obviously not)? Hence, English class being so special. I felt comfortable there because I knew it was where I belonged. I was in my element. Being on set gave me that same feeling. When you're the sister of one of the stars, everyone is nice to you. I didn't have to worry about being judged or not fitting in.

We were in Minden for three months, and my dad and the twins came after three weeks to stay the rest of the time. My parents enrolled the twins in a local preschool run by Keke's football coach hired by the film to teach her how to throw properly. We were staying in what was originally a two-story hotel, but then my mom was bitten by a brown recluse spider. It destroyed the tissue on her leg surrounding the bite, so naturally none of us wanted to continue sleeping there. They moved us into a huge house somewhere in Shreveport, and for a while it felt like *this* was home.

But it wasn't, and we were packing our bags to go back to Los Angeles before I knew it. The plane from Shreveport back to Dallas was still small, but there were two rows of seats on each side of the aisle this time. I sat with my brother, Lawrence, while Keke sat with Lawrencia. My parents sat together. It was cloudy, but there wasn't any rain or anything. It was just a normal situation—until it wasn't. Suddenly, this plane started dropping. My brother looked at me and said, "It's like a rollercoaster!"

"Yeah," was my response. I didn't even look at him. Instead, I tried not to panic, and looked for anyone in my family who could calm me down, say that it would be okay. They all had the audacity to sleep through it. We stopped dropping for a moment, then started dropping again. Lawrence was throwing his damn hands up in the air and giggling. I wanted to vomit. I looked at the flight attendant for reassurance. She caught my eye, and I realized by how high her eyebrows were raised and the thin straight line that should have been her lips that she had been searching for someone to do the same for her.

Then the damn plane started to shake from side to side. I just *knew* this would wake someone up, and it did...just not anyone in *my* family. Now everyone on the plane (except the other Palmers) was up and worried. I felt like I was going to die. I *knew* I was going to die. I did something that I hadn't done in a long time: I prayed. I am ashamed to say that as a practicing Catholic, *this* was the first time I had prayed in a long time. My church family would be shocked. With tears in my eyes, I asked God to let me walk off this plane. I promised to be kind, to study hard, to respect my parents, to be a good big sister, to keep my room clean—basically the same stuff I prayed for as a kid when Devil Kazuya would kick my ass in *Tekken 2*.

Obviously, I didn't die. The plane landed, I got off, and my dad had to force me to get on the next flight from Dallas back to LA. He wasn't having my dramatics. I reluctantly got on and vowed to never set foot on a plane again. I can count the flights I've taken since then on one hand: one was to my grandmother's funeral, the other was to President Barack Obama's inaugural ball, another was to visit Keke while filming in Budapest, and the last was to Cancun for a music festival Keke was hosting. I use Amtrak these days to get where I need to go.

So, once again, I was back in LA. I registered for a math class over the summer, but I never showed up for the final and failed. I was no longer interested. By this point, I had convinced myself that school was all wrong. I loved English and writing, but the idea of prerequisites in math and science nauseated me. Immediately no. I registered for spring, but rarely showed up and again failed, again due to lack of interest. I was entering my "lost" era. Keke had started filming *True Jackson, VP* for Nickelodeon, and Stage 25 on the Paramount backlot had become a second home—actually, it had become a *first* home. I knew I liked to tell stories, and it was around this time that I thought maybe I wanted to tell stories for the silver screen. Again, I hated the idea of prerequisites. I just wanted to learn what *I* wanted to learn. School was no longer doing it for me.

I withdrew from all my classes but wasn't stupid enough to tell my parents this. I had made a huge deal of being all about school, and now here I was dropping out. I found the silver lining: I would just transfer. That's what they expected you to do at a community college anyway. I searched online for film schools that I could get into with my horrific grades. I found one with few admission standards, if any, but access to equipment, which was what I really needed. Its big selling point was that you could rent equipment as a student and start filming day one. I signed myself right up.

I had this new fantasy of becoming the next Wes Craven. I wanted to learn screenwriting and directing so that I could make indie horror movies like the ones I'd grown up on, maybe even someday open my own film production company that only dealt with horror and all its glorious subgenres. I spent the weeks leading up to the first day of term soaking in every documentary on making a horror movie I could find. I hadn't even started my first class, but I was already thinking about my thesis film. One of the documentaries I watched featured serial killers and how viewers become obsessed with unpacking what led them down that path. I was going to make a traditional '80s slasher film, set in the '80s, about a notorious serial killer. I was even thinking about the soundtrack, which would of course be '80s inspired, complete with guitar riffs and all. I could already see it in my head.

A few weeks before school started, I got cold feet. Even though I had been at PCC for two years, I still wasn't good at socializing with people my own age. In my mind, I just wasn't where they were. To me, they were real adults, with real jobs, and real relationships. Even my younger sister had had her first kiss by this time, and I'd never even held a man's hand. I was inferior. I wasn't a real adult. I felt like I had paused socially in the ninth grade. All the growth adolescents experience during high school had passed me by. I wanted to stay at home, my safe place, and just take some online film courses. I called my admissions rep and broke the news. She sounded so disappointed. She did her best to convince me to take the plunge, but my mind was made up. I thanked her for her time, real professional-like, and hung up the phone. I didn't know what to tell my parents. I was a failure in so many ways.

Later that night, while I was watching *American Dad*, an email alert popped across my computer screen. It was my admissions rep. I expected some official paperwork that acknowledged I had withdrawn from the school. What I got was a heartfelt email about change, and how scary it can be. "All things change, but not all change is bad," she wrote.

I thought about the other big changes I'd experienced in life. I recalled being forced into that stupid Dodge Caravan to drive across the country. I recalled our first years in Hollywood that were filled with cheap motels and ninety-nine-cent-store groceries, the family dinners in our stuffy two-bedroom apartment, and attending my dad's company baseball games. As I looked around my bedroom in the new million-dollar home my parents had just purchased in Pasadena, I recalled the good things that had happened as a result of that change: all the travel, the award shows, meeting Mariska Hargitay! I had experienced things that most people only dream about (tragic serenity!). I got to hang out on studio lots that were home to some of my favorite shows growing up, I got to meet John Stamos (Uncle Jessie), accompany Keke on tour with the Jonas Brothers, spend Thanksgiving Day with Robin Williams on set as he told so many jokes it was hard to keep the meal down. I had changed inside as well; seeing my sister accomplish so much, so young, made me feel like nothing was outside of the realm of possibility. If she can do it, so can I.

I responded to her email with six words: *See you in a few weeks*.

During my first week, the three-member team of instructors for the intro course literally put a camera in my hand and said, "Make a film." I hate to admit this, but I was a total film snob. The past few years of my life had been spent on film sets, and I had this fantastical idea that simply being there had somehow rubbed off some knowledge onto me—plus I wanted to impress the other students. I wanted them to see that I was a visionary—only I wasn't. The first week was a group assignment, and I convinced my group to film my idea. While it wasn't awful, it also wasn't good (okay, maybe it was awful). We had to make a film about something that was lost and then found again in one continuous shot. I chose to have a girl drawing in a sketchbook. Then when she got up to leave, the sketchbook fell out of her backpack. As she searched for it, a Disney executive found it and offered her a job—don't judge me.

The school ran on a system where every month you learned a new element of film: month one was an overview, two was history of film, three was editing, then production, and so on, so each month was a new course. The next month, I was determined to step it up. I was going to be amazing. This course was called "The Art of Film and Video." It was basically a history course for film. It wasn't as exciting as putting a camera into my hand, but it was still interesting. Up until that point, my knowledge of film history had only consisted of films I had seen (and my horror documentaries) and the bits and pieces of information I had haphazardly collected being on sets. Now I was learning about filmmakers in Italy, Japan, India—all over the world.

If I was a film snob before, this was making it worse. Halfway through the course, our instructors let us know that we would be making our first short film. This one needed an actual script, and we had to assign jobs and hire real actors. It wasn't meant to be great. In fact, it was expected to be awful. The point was to put what we had learned to the test, and ultimately be able to look back at the end of the program to see how far we'd come. My film brain went to work again, and I was already thinking of the many ways I could prove I was meant to be a writer/director. I had about five ideas in my notebook when the instructor announced, "Okay, everybody get into groups."

In the previous course, we had been assigned groups. Now, we had to pick people to partner with. Panicking, I searched around the room for someone who looked even remotely welcoming. There was a group next to me that was short one person. Before my brain could stop me, my mouth blurted out, "Can I join you guys?" The girl just stared at me, looking as if I had just asked for her firstborn. Another guy started to walk over, and he looked as if he was going to ask to join. I guess I was the better option of the two, because when he finally did ask, she told him they were full and slid over to make room for me.

We had about fifteen minutes or so to come up with an idea. I shared mine. No one hated it, but no one loved it either. There were ten of us, and after idea number nine, none of us were excited about anything yet. Then the last guy started to speak. His voice was soft yet commanding. He wasn't really my type, but he was cute. What really caught my attention was how passionate he was when he spoke about his idea. His eyes lit up, and the corner of his mouth twitched when he started talking about a part he was really excited about. His idea was great, and it was the one we picked. It was about a guy who had a crush on the new coworker, but he was too shy to say anything about it. That night, he would have a series of dreams about introducing himself to her, finally, but each dream would take place in a different film genre (horror, western, 1950s, black-and-white).

After class, half of us decided to walk to Denny's on Gower to discuss the project some more. The guy whose idea we had picked came along, but he just sat quietly and didn't say much. In fact, I talked to everyone else more than I talked to him.

I was so excited about the idea and the role I had been assigned: production designer (no one voted for me to be the director or the screenwriter, but I digress). Later that night, I was doing a Google search on how to "dress a scene" when a Facebook alert came through. I had received a friend request from Frank Wimberly. It was *him*. I accepted his request and began to Facebook stalk him. He was a nerd. A horror nerd. A cute horror nerd. His page was full of images from *Resident Evil* and *Saw*, two of my favorite horror franchises at the time. As I was on his page, he posted something about watching his favorite *Saw* film to get to bed. I commented, and we kept going back and forth for what seemed like just a few minutes but was actually over an hour.

We didn't have long to work on this "film." Less than thirty days. None of us knew what the hell we were doing. Despite my years of hanging out on sets with Keke, I was essentially useless when it came to the mechanics of filmmaking. I can say that now, but at the time I really thought we were making movie magic. At some point we were forced to grapple with the fact that we couldn't act in this thing ourselves. We had to hire actors. One of us posted a casting call on the websites our instructors suggested, and then we held auditions. It ended up being Frank, myself, and the other girl in the group holding the auditions. We were the camera department, and a production designer.

During that process, Frank and I got to know each other more. He seemed to genuinely enjoy my lame jokes, and we had the same taste in horror movies. We both loved the bad ones. I mean the really, really bad ones. The ones where you have to stop and ask yourself, who greenlit this? After the auditions, he invited me over to his apartment in Los Angeles off of Western Ave to borrow some of his favorite horror movies that I hadn't seen. I'd heard of them, I just hadn't gotten around to them. I remember one was *The Collector*. As we got closer to his place, I could tell he was getting nervous because he started to fidget in his seat as he played with his jacket zipper. Before we turned down his street, he felt the need to give me a disclaimer.

"It's really small, and the area isn't great. I don't have much furniture."

I smiled. "I'm sure it's just fine."

I'd never been materialistic. He could've lived in a hut, and I wouldn't have cared—although I would've had a lot of questions regarding the electricity and plumbing situation.

We pulled up to his building, and I found nothing wrong with his apartment. Yes, the area was considered shady to a lot of people, but if he had seen where I came from (which he eventually would) he'd have skipped the disclaimer altogether. He was on the first floor, all the way in the back. When he opened the door, my first thought wasn't, "Gee, this place is small," but, "Wow! He has his own place!" I was still living at home with my parents, who were totally cool, but still my parents. Twenty-two was creeping up, and I was itching for independence. I liked living with my family, but I couldn't do so *forever*.

The studio was small, but he had made it look homey. The black futon sat in the middle of the floor with a fluffy gray blanket folded across the back. He had two pillows tucked into each armrest. There was a huge flatscreen TV sitting on a stand that was probably an inch or two too small. He had one lone shelf, maybe four feet tall and wide. On its side was a 007 sticker that covered it completely. I didn't go into his kitchen, but what I could see looked clean. The closet was wide open and full of movies. It was a good thing he claimed not to have many clothes, because the closet was the length of the wall, and most of it was filled with DVDs and Blu-rays.

He offered me a soda and apologized that he only had a futon to offer me for seating (little did he know, I, too, was sleeping on a futon—by choice). We made small talk, nothing deep or romantic, but I still felt a connection. Historically, I had made talking to the opposite sex a scary adventure. Yet here I was talking to a guy. And it wasn't awkward! It was even comfortable. Extremely comfortable. I was enjoying myself, bonding over our shared interest.

It was starting to get late, so he went to his movie shelf and picked out the eight titles we had discussed. I stood up to grab the movies, and he pulled out this weird tiny backpack and wrapped them inside a slightly bigger cloth backpack with a buckle.

"Don't worry, I will guard them with my life," I joked in a mock serious voice. To which he responded, "Yeah, I'm just a real freak about the cases. I don't like them getting smudged or scratched."

I laughed, and that was that. We went our separate ways, and I vowed to watch the movies within the next two weeks. That night I went home and unpacked the movies. I laid them out on the desk in my room and climbed into my futon to go to bed. For the first time in a while, I started to think that maybe going on a date wouldn't be such a bad thing.

The next morning, I woke up to my beagle, Rascal, chewing something on my bed. He was always chewing something, so I didn't think twice. I was running late, so I took a five-minute shower and threw myself together. On the way out, I went to give Rascal a kiss goodbye and saw what he was chewing—one of Frank's fucking precious movies. By the time I noticed, he was already halfway through the case. I was completely pan-icked. I had finally found a guy I was interested in getting to know better, who seemed like he was possibly interested in getting to know me. Then here comes dumbass Rascal and chews up one of his precious DVDs. I couldn't do anything about it now. The damage was done. I went to class, and when I saw Frank, I didn't say anything. I *couldn't* say anything. After class, I confided to a friend in our group what happened. We decided that the most responsible thing to do would be to replace the case and take this secret to our graves.

The school was located near Amoeba Music, a hipster record store that also had a big collection of obscure movies. So we walked over, found the same one Rascal had chewed up, and went home to make the transfer. When we got to my house (where my bedroom door was now locked and a Rascal-free zone), we ran upstairs to put the old disc into the new case. There was just one problem—the case for the film that I had just purchased was noticeably wider than the original. Panicking, we decided to try Blockbuster (RIP, Blockbuster). It took three locations before we found the right case (we took the original along this time for comparison). It was a perfect match (years later he told me it wasn't, but he never said anything).

After that incident, most of our hangouts started as meetings about our short film and ended with us watching a horror movie from his collection back at his place. Meanwhile, the script for our "movie" was finally complete, and now we had to start shooting. Looking back, we were nowhere near as productive as we should have been. The meetings rarely lasted more than thirty minutes, and most of the time less than half of our group even showed up, but we really thought we were filmmakers. One night, after our "crew meeting," Frank mentioned the new *Resident Evil* movie was coming out.

"Yeah, I know, I'm super excited!"

"There's a midnight showing at City Walk," he threw out casually. "Wanna go?"

"Yeah, that'll be fun."

To prepare for the showing, we decided to marathon the preceding three films that night. We had barely made it through the second film when sleep started calling my name. He walked me to my car, and we said our goodbyes. There was still nothing romantic regarding our exchange, despite my wanting there to be, so I didn't think anything of it when I told Keke and her friends. They were the ones who told me it was a date. A date. I both wanted and *feared* a date.

"Make sure you dress cute!"

"If he puts the armrest down, then he's not that interested."

"If he keeps it up, that means he might try something."

Try what? I liked Frank, but I wasn't ready for a guy to "try something" with me. How would I even respond? What would I even do? At this point, I had to go to an expert: my dad. He was a guy, so he should know how to anticipate a guy's moves on a date, right? Wrong.

"Dad, how do I know if a guy has asked me out on a date?"

"Did he ask you out and say it was a date?"

"Dad, what? No, he didn't say date, but he asked to go to the movies."

"Does he like you?"

"I don't know, but does this mean he does?

"Not necessarily," he said with a straight face.

"Well, how do I find out?"

"You have to ask him, Lori."

"Keke said if he puts the arm rest down, it's not a date."

His face frowned up. "That's crazy. Don't listen to that. Look, you just have to straight-up ask him. Is this a date?" He emphasized this with open arms waving at his sides.

"There's no other way to find out?"

"You could tell *him* it's a date."

I thanked him for all of his help and left his room.

If I had been sixteen and going through this, maybe I would've been able to calm my nerves. Maybe my excitement wouldn't have bordered on terror. But I was turning twenty-two in three months, and by my age most people had gone through the uncomfortableness of their first date. By this age, I was expected (in my mind) to know how to conduct myself on a date, to know how to handle the moment when a guy *tried something*.

I decided to talk about it with a friend from film school who found himself in the same exact position as me. Never been on a date, and never been kissed. Our date-virgin minds came up with an obvious solution. He would go with us, since he knew Frank too. He'd sit on the opposite side of me, one seat away. That way we could go on our date, but I'd have the safety of someone being with me in case he tried something I wasn't ready for.

I didn't think to tell Frank I was bringing a friend. I didn't think it mattered. *He* had never used the word date, and you have to actually use the word when it's a real date, right? I picked up my friend, and then we met Frank at the school. When he saw me, he began to smile and waved me over. I parked, and when I got out of the car he was still smiling, until my friend hopped out of the passenger seat. I immediately saw him deflate, and I knew I had ruined everything. Once we made it over to where he was standing, he perked up, and he greeted him warmly.

"I didn't know you were coming," he said to my friend, looking back and forth between the two of us.

"Well, Loreal's been telling me about these movies, and you're obsessed with Milla Jovovich, so I figured it might be worth the watch," my friend chimed in.

Frank smiled. I couldn't even speak. I was so embarrassed.

The plan was to meet at the school, then take the train to City Walk. My friend promised to walk behind us and pretend to be engaged in a deep text conversation. Frank and I walked together down Sunset Boulevard. We didn't hold hands, but we were very close, and he was more animated than usual. I started to think that maybe I hadn't blown it after all. We were in our own little world. There was no flirting, but *something* was happening, and it annoyed us both when my friend popped up behind us and interrupted our conversation.

"Question," he started, "how are we getting home? Does the train run late here?"

The thought had never crossed my mind. I lived in Pasadena, unlike everyone else we went to school with who all lived fairly close, so I always needed a car to get around in a timely manner. I guess Frank had never considered it either, because he looked just as clueless as I was.

"I guess we can just take my car," I offered.

We walked quickly back the way we came and stuffed ourselves into my little two-door 2001 Chevy Cavalier (it was fine for two people, but any more than that and it got uncomfortable). There was traffic, and I could see Frank was getting anxious. I glanced at the clock.

"We'll make good time," I offered.

He continued looking out of the window.

"Yeah, but I was hoping we'd make the coming attractions."

I glanced in the rearview mirror and saw my friend staring out of his window extremely uninterested. This was such a huge mistake. I just wanted it to be over.

We arrived at City Walk, and of course parking was limited. We were far. Really far. We had to practically run to make the film on time, let alone any coming attractions. When we arrived at the kiosk, we each paid for our own tickets. *So, it isn't a date?* There was no time for snacks (my favorite part), so we went straight to our theater. It was crowded, so my friend ended up sitting right next to me. We settled in about ten minutes after the movie had started. I noticed, however, that Frank didn't put the armrest down. *Is it a date?* It didn't matter because before I knew it, my friend was nudging me to tell me that I was snoring.

"You were really loud."

I peeked over at Frank who seemed like he had no clue what was going on. I figured he had been exaggerating, and maybe I could stay up now after the quick power nap. Wrong. I didn't see any of the movie that night, and the next time I opened my eyes, it was 2:00 a.m. and the lights were coming on in the theater.

"How did you like it?" I asked him.

"It was great! I can't wait until it's out on Blu-ray." Then he added, laughing, "You can watch it then."

I was mortified.

Frank smiled.

The plan had been to drive them home after the movie, but it was two o'clock in the morning, and I was exhausted.

"Did anyone check to see about the trains, or the buses?"

Neither of them had.

"I thought you were dropping us off?" My friend asked, shocked.

I didn't know what to do. I was so exhausted I didn't even know if I could safely take myself home.

"I'm really tired," I tried to explain.

"Well, you slept the whole movie, so you should be well rested," he shot back.

Frank just stood quietly, watching the exchange take place.

"I'm all the way in Pasadena, if I take you guys home, I have to go in the complete opposite direction, then come all the way back. I don't think I can."

My friend was gearing up to say something, but Frank interjected. "It's fine, I'm sure the train will be coming soon. We can just wait here together. Get home safely."

We didn't hug, and I couldn't even look at my friend. I just walked away. I must've swerved all the way home; my eyes were fighting to stay open as I ran damn near every red light to get to my bed. When I finally did get home, I didn't even bother undressing. I just got straight under the covers, too exhausted to think about how I'd blown my first date ever.

The next morning, I walked into class and my friend was deliberately ignoring me. I asked him what time he got home, and he spat out 5:00 a.m. I apologized profusely.

"Well, I appreciate your apology, but you should know I said a lot of bad things to my mom about you."

I thought he was joking. He wasn't.

I shrugged and we went on about our morning. We stayed friends for a while after that, but our friendship was never the same. I ran into Frank shortly after, and he was normal. In fact, he was more than normal—he was genuinely excited to see me. Other than mentioning the lack of sleep, he seemed completely unbothered by last night. He kept talking, but I couldn't tell you what about, because all I could think about from that point on was how much I really, really liked him.

My mom would always tell me that I'd find someone when I least expected to. I wasn't even thinking about a guy at this point. I was so involved in my filmmaking dream that had I not been in his group, I doubt I would've met Frank. I hadn't recognized him before. There was another Frank in our class that I recognized more. I felt like that meant it *had* to be fate. I wasn't looking, and *he* came to *me*. Prince Charming came to the Princess.

That meant this would be real, right?

9

Love Island

I won't bore you with every little detail of Frank and I becoming an actual couple, but that's what happened next. One night, while driving to his apartment after class, like we'd done a million times before, I just asked him.

"What are we?"

His mouth did that little twitching it did when he was uncomfortable. I had caught him off guard.

"What do you want us to be?"

I shrugged, feeling a jolt of nervous excitement, before answering sheepishly, "I'd like you to be my boyfriend."

This time, it was Frank's turn to smile.

"Then you're my girlfriend."

He grabbed my hand, and we continued down Western Ave, oblivious to all the ridiculousness that usually caused our fury during the forty-five-minute drive to his apartment. We were in our own little world, but it didn't last long. Once word got out that we were a couple, we were met with opposition from his friends. None of them thought we'd last. They didn't think I was good enough for him.

In film school, you have your film snobs who only watch films recommended by the academy. Then you have those who watch movies simply for enjoyment. I was in the latter group. I could enjoy *Snakes on a Plane* and *The Godfather* back-to-back. A film didn't have to win awards to be worthy of my time. But it did to them, and that made my taste, and by extension *me*, inferior.

Here I was, at the ripe old age of twenty-one, with my first boyfriend ever, and I was playing tug-of-war for Frank's attention. His friends liked to go see black-and-white films at specialty theaters, while I was perfectly happy at his place, binging the entire *Nightmare on Elm Street* franchise while eating pretzel-crust cheese pizza. Frank liked to do both and was torn between hanging out with me and his cinephile film school friends. Our first few fights were born of this tension.

Our school hosted free film screenings every Friday, and during October they were all horror movies leading up to Halloween. The first one was *A Nightmare on Elm Street*. Perfect, right? Of course, Frank and I were going together. The plan was to part ways after class, then meet up about an hour before the movie started to get in line for seats. I had a good friend, Jovon, whom I'd met in the industry. His mom was an amazingly talented hairstylist who had worked with Keke. Although he didn't attend school with us, he was a total horror fan and knew some of the other students going. He had acted in a short for us, and I thought it would be awesome to invite him (are we sensing a pattern here?). Frank, apparently, had the same idea and invited his friend Denice, whom we both knew from school. I also knew that she hated me, probably because she liked Frank. Or maybe she didn't hate me at all. I don't think about her or this time much, but when I do (from my distanced lens) I feel like I could've been the problem—a.k.a. I *was* the problem. I was new to dating, and I assumed she was competition. She was much older than us (late twenties), and in my mind that made her the more desirable. I'd always heard that guys were into older girls. I assumed she had experience.

When my friend and I arrived, I texted Frank. When he didn't respond, I had my friend hold our place in line while I walked to see if maybe he was further behind in the line. Then I walked towards the front and saw him, with her, engaged in an extremely animated conversation. At twenty-one, I was very insecure, and the sight of my brand-new boyfriend talking to another girl seemed like a huge threat. I immediately went back to my friend and told him what I'd seen. Wrong move, because he was ready to act up with me. There was no voice of reason here, at all. We decided that we were going to sit as far away from them as possible. When the doors opened, we walked all the way to the back of the theater. I knew Frank would sit near the center for the best sound. I saw him looking around for me. For a moment, we made eye contact. He smiled, and waved me over, pointing to two empty seats next to them. If looks could kill, Frank would have been dead on arrival. Before the lights went out, I saw his face deflate. The poor guy had no idea what he'd done wrong. Sadly, neither did I.

After storming out of there, I drove myself home. I don't even remember watching the movie. By the time I had undressed and gotten into bed, my phone had at least ten texts from Frank asking what was going on. I let him have it (so dramatic). I accused him of wanting to see the movie with *her* and not me. He apologized, genuinely confused, and told me he'd saved me a seat. I rationalized the situation by texting:

I at least told you my friend was coming. You just showed up with someone—a girl.

I waited bitchily for his response.

I ran into her and told her we were going, and she wanted to come too. I didn't think it was a big deal.

The thing is, it wasn't a big deal. At all. But I wanted it to be. It was like I was craving the relationship dramatics I'd grown up watching play out in teen dramas. Looking back, I can see just how crazy I was about some of it (a lot of it). But Frank wasn't completely innocent. Not too long after, he was supposed to meet me for a lunch date. I waited over an hour, just for him to show up after my lunch was over, to tell me that he had gone to help Denice look for some horror-themed calendar at a store she'd found on Hollywood Boulevard. She couldn't remember which store it had been exactly, so the quick ten-minute trip grew. His phone was dead, so he couldn't reach me to tell me to go eat without him. After that, I gave him an ultimatum.

"She likes you. You have to know that," I blurted out on one of our drives to his place.

"But I don't like her," he sighed. "So what does it matter if she likes me?"

"Well, she doesn't like me, and I wouldn't hang out with someone who didn't like you," I reasoned.

It gets tricky here, because I have no idea whether she liked me or not, but at this point, I was not very friendly to her, thanks to my own insecurities and my friends reinforcing them. I had to stake my claim, and the hot-and-cold way I treated her wasn't welcoming at all. But that didn't register then. All that mattered was that I kept my boyfriend.

"If it upsets you, then, I'll stop seeing her."

I grabbed his hand. I was satisfied for all of ten minutes (really a few months), because I found out that they had still been seeing each other, and this only fed my paranoia, because it turned out I wasn't paranoid after all.

Weeks later, Frank was getting ready to go to some college-film-awards event, and he wanted me to be at his place when he came home, so I told him I'd stay. He looked so handsome and was excited. He'd been waiting for this event for months. When his ride came to pick him up, he kissed me goodbye before telling me to order whatever I wanted, and that he'd eat whatever I picked for him. I got settled onto his futon and started to examine his large Blu-ray collection. It had grown considerably since I'd met him. The poor shelf was starting to buckle. The little shoebox apartment he had once been so ashamed of was really starting to come together. He'd added a kitchen table, a nicer futon, a better TV. He was slowly making Los Angeles his home. He wasn't the quiet boy from Tucson who kept to himself anymore.

I was looking for a good horror movie to watch when his laptop pinged with a Facebook notification. Most people would have minded their own business and moved on with their day, but I'm not most people. I opened it and saw it was a message from *her*. I opened the chat window and saw that they'd been having daily conversations—long ones. In one thread, he had even insinuated that he wanted to kiss her. I also saw that the day he told me he was too sick to go see *Insidious* with me, he had gone to see it with Denice. In fact, after some detective work that would make Scooby-Doo proud, I found out that every time he had told me he was unable to hang, he was doing something with *her*.

My drama mode had been activated. I felt like Topanga from *Boy Meets World* after she found out Cory had kissed Lauren on the ski trip. I didn't even wait for Frank to come home. I couldn't. Through tears, nice big dramatic ones, I texted him that I hated him. That he was a cheater. That I was glad we hadn't had sex yet, because he didn't deserve to have sex with me. I told him I was leaving, and that he shouldn't even bother reaching out to me because we were absolutely done. I was in the car, playing Carrie Underwood and singing through my tears along to "Before He Cheats," when his texts came through begging me to stay so that we could talk.

I'd started the car and was just about to drive home, when something told me to hear Frank out. I felt so hurt and betrayed that I wanted to run away, but I also felt like I should hear him out. The truth was, I didn't want this relationship to end. I wanted him to apologize, and for things go back to normal. I wasn't ready for my first relationship to end.

I only had to wait for about thirty minutes before Frank pulled up to his apartment building. I was ready to let him have it, but I decided to let him speak first. I thought, let's hear his excuse before we poke holes in it. Imagine my surprise when the first words that came out of his mouth were, "You ruined my entire night. This was the most exciting thing I'd ever gotten to be a part of, and from the moment I saw your texts, it was ruined."

I was speechless. The tone of his texts was not this. I did not stay for *this*. I let him finish, as he next moved on to how I invaded his privacy. Now I was ready.

"I probably should've just closed your laptop, but I'm glad I didn't. You are a liar!" I shouted. "You're still seeing her!"

"I don't have any friends here, Loreal," he said defensively. "I don't get along well with other guys, and you're trying to take away the one real friend I've made since moving here. I can't always hang out with you!"

I wasn't listening. "Well, you also don't have to hang out with just her. And, if you're telling her you want to kiss her while she's 'wearing only an apron,' that suggests more than a friendship!"

He flinched. Apparently, he didn't think I'd gone back that far in their message thread, but I had. Seeing that notification pop up had opened a rabbit hole that I had fully explored. Frank's anger melted as he realized all I had seen. He had thought I'd only seen the messages from that day. It hadn't dawned on him that I would keep scrolling.

"It was just a stupid joke," he said, struggling for words as he took off his suit jacket.

I stood firm. "Then why are you still even talking to her when you said you wouldn't?"

"I told Denice that we couldn't be friends anymore, but she convinced me we could still hang out, and that if you didn't know, you wouldn't get upset." He looked scared. "I promise I don't like her in that way at all. I just wanted a friend."

"I saw the conversations, Frank. You guys talked about a lot of deep stuff. You ditched me to hang with her. You say you never kissed her, but you still cheated. You emotionally cheated."

"Please don't say that. It wasn't like that."

He stepped closer, and I stepped back.

"But it was. That's what you did."

114

He never looked at it that way. It was a friendship to him—and knowing what I *now* know, I can see that it really was. We went on like that for a good hour, maybe more. Ultimately, he agreed that he wouldn't talk to her anymore. This time he really didn't.

Their interactions following that conversation were awkward at best. More so on her part than Frank's. He was professional and cordial in classes with her, but she would obviously avoid him, making a spectacle by walking all the way around the classroom when it would have been easier to just walk past him. If they were assigned a task together, she would avoid eye contact, deliberately looking at the floor or off to the side any time he spoke. I could tell it was upsetting Frank, but I didn't care. I believed that there was a romantic connection between the two of them, and I just wanted that to end.

They couldn't continue to sneak around behind my back and make jokes about it over Facebook Messenger. He couldn't continue to have two relationships with two completely different women. I'll never know if it was just a friendship for her, but I'm convinced that maybe it wasn't. Maybe she, too, had been entranced by the magic that was Frank. This perfect, sweet, soft-spoken guy who loved horror movies, *Star Wars*, and anime. Maybe all the things I'd fallen for, she'd fallen for too. I knew Frank was lonely, and that even the most committed introverts needed friends, but *I* was his friend. In my mind, I was the only female companion he needed.

Graduation came quickly, and by that point I really didn't think about the other girl anymore. Not trying to be rude, but a few months had passed since then, and it all felt like a distant memory. Frank had made new friends (new guy friends), and as far as I was concerned, all was well in the world. Well, almost. Now that the nice security blanket of film school was ending, we had to actually go out into the real world and be functioning adults. I was starting to become afraid again. What if I couldn't get a job? What if Frank couldn't get a job? What if not seeing me all day everyday made him realize he didn't want to be with me? What if, what if, what *if*? Worrying about every little thing that could possibly go wrong with us, I almost "what-iffed" myself to death.

That's when I made up my mind. We had to get married. If I really wanted to start a life with Frank, I had to start a life with him, *all* the way. We had to be all in. So, I started dropping hints, showing him pictures of different engagement rings that I thought were pretty—you know, "just because." I had surpassed hinting, that was too subtle for my style. Around that same time, I started looking for jobs that we could both do together, to keep our momentum going. We were in a good place, and I was afraid of losing that connection. We worked on a few shorts together, then a TV pilot, but the work wasn't steady. That didn't stop the fantasy world I had created from running 24/7 in my head. I was getting married, and I was going to live happily ever after—even if it killed us both.

The winter following graduation, Frank told me that he wanted to take me to his home in Tucson, Arizona, for Christmas. To me, it was the perfect next step for blending our families. It wouldn't be long before a proposal now. So far, I'd only met Frank's family once. It was just after we had started dating, and his mother, Margaret, had come to Los Angles with his brothers for his birthday. His youngest brother, Michael, was charming, his other brother, Tony, was quiet. His mom was...interesting. She had told Frank they would arrive at 9:00

a.m. sharp. He was so excited. I told him that I'd come over at 10:00, so that I wasn't bombarding everyone all at once.

I pulled up at ten o'clock that morning with my best outfit on and my hair bone straight. I was determined to make a good first impression. I knocked on his door and was surprised to see that Frank was all alone when he opened it.

"Where is everyone?" I asked.

"They got a late start. They'll be here around noon," was all he replied as he moved out of the way to let me in. He wasn't a messy guy, but the place was spotless. He had a sugar cookie candle burning in the kitchen, and the warm scent had filled the room. He had new dishes organized into place settings on the dining table and a new rug centered in the living room area that was tucked slightly underneath the fancy futon. He, too, wanted to make a good impression.

We watched movies as noon came and went. He called his mom a few times, trying not to reveal to me just how upset he was. At some point in the afternoon, I suggested we go out to pick up his birthday gift. I knew there were a few movies he had been eyeing, so I decided I'd take him to Best Buy so that we could pick them up. The whole trip took about an hour or so. As we left the store, he tried to call his mom a few more times, but there was no answer. I was getting worried. What if they had gotten into an accident on the road?

"Nothing's wrong with them," he shrugged. "She always does stuff like this. I don't know why I expected anything different."

We got back in the car and started driving in silence. We passed one of our favorite local Mexican restaurants. It was now well after 6:00 p.m., so I said, "Turn around, let's get dinner." We ordered all our favorite dishes and decided we would go back to his place, curl up on the futon, and watch his new movies. His mood was brighter, and he was back to his usual silly self, making goofy dad jokes and tickling me at random just to hear me snort. By the time we pulled up in front of his apartment complex, we had forgotten his mother and brothers were even coming—until they pulled up right behind us.

His mom got out of the car, and she already seemed annoyed. She didn't even wish Frank a happy birthday. "I'm here," she announced. As if she was being grotesquely inconvenienced. They all seemed miserable.

"What did you get us?" Margaret asked, peering into the bag of takeout.

Frank pulled it away. "What did you get *me*?" he asked. "It's *my* birthday."

His mother looked at him with her piercing brown eyes and a facial expression that suggested he had insulted her.

"I'm here?"

She phrased it like a question. Like, "hello?" Or "duh." Frank rolled his eyes and led everyone into the house. There wasn't enough food for five people, so I pretended not to be hungry (I was starving) so that there was enough food for everybody. Frank shared his plate with me. The entire time, Margaret and Tony ignored me. They never looked at me, never asked a single question about me or my life, never even acknowledged my presence. If it hadn't been for Michael and Frank, I would have started to wonder if I was invisible, or more so, I would feel how I felt on those early days of set life, that there was an invisible club here that I just didn't belong to.

After dinner, I told Frank I was leaving. This was awful and I didn't want to be there any longer.

"Why can't they just get a hotel, and we have our own celebration?" I asked, all annoying and pouty.

"They can't afford it."

I felt awful, but I was committed to playing my role. I rolled my eyes, resigned to the night ending prematurely. He walked me to my car and kissed me good night before going in for the kill.

"I probably won't see you again until they leave."

"What?" I turned around, "Why *not*?"

Frank looked at the ground, trying hard to avoid my eyes—he knew I was staring into him.

"I just think it's best."

"Whatever," I said as I got into my car and started the engine.

He looked sad as he watched me get in. "Can I call you tomorrow?"

"Nope." I drove off, confused, pissed, and devastated all at once.

None of that mattered anymore though, because I was going to be family soon. Frank's mother would just have to learn to love me.

Following the traumatic flight experience from Shreveport to Dallas while Keke was filming *The Longshots*, I had developed an intense fear of flying, so we decided to drive to Arizona. I'm always up for a good road trip, and I was genuinely excited for the eight-hour drive. Just us, our snacks, and conversation. What I'm about to describe might sound crazy, but Frank and I both swear we saw an alien spacecraft land in the desert. Let me explain. It was around midnight; we had been on the road for hours, and we were both exhausted. As we were driving along a dark and lonely stretch of highway in the middle of nowhere, suddenly a bright green streak of light shot across the sky and then hit the ground somewhere in the distance. I stared at the horizon in stunned silence for a few seconds before I could get my mouth to form words.

"Frank, did you...did you see that?" I asked.

"Yup," was all he said as he stepped on the gas and sped up.

We were silent for the next ten or so miles. We passed the "You are Now Entering Tucson" sign and got off at our exit. Frank started to get excited. He'd been rather quiet the latter half of the trip, probably because I'd been either asleep or cranky—or maybe it was because of our ET sighting. Driving through his old neighborhood, Frank showed me all his favorite spots: Bookman's, his local bookstore; Eegee's, a slushy and fast-food spot; and his high school, where he had gotten his act together at the last minute to graduate on time.

As we got closer to his mother's house, Frank's mood began to shift. A dark cloud settled over us, and he started to get somber.

"We don't live the way you do, just so you know," he finally said. "Don't expect much."

He was so worried that I would scoff at the duplex where his family lived because it wasn't the huge house my parents had. It was the apartment explanation all over again. Little did he know, the neighborhood we were driving through looked pretty good compared to where we had grown up in Robbins, Illinois. People I met during the years after *True Jackson, VP* always assumed that the nice house my family lived in was how I'd always lived. I was almost fifteen when I left Illinois. That's a lot of years of lower middle-class/poor living, plus things didn't really take off for Keke until I was around seventeen or eighteen. I didn't grow up in a mansion in Pasadena. This shit was new to me too!

"I'm sure it's fine," I said, squeezing his hand. "Don't let how my family lives now fool you."

We pulled up to his mom's duplex, and it was the kind of home I could see myself living in. She had a little patio set up on the side of the house and lots of desert plants surrounding her walkway. I was less anxious about Frank's mom than I was about his brothers. Frank loved his brothers. I really wanted to impress them. I wanted them to think, "Wow! Frank's girlfriend is so cool!" I'd always imagined myself being best friends with my future mother-in-law. I knew by then that this was unlikely, but the sibling friendship was still on the table, I hoped.

When we arrived, his brothers, who were two and three years younger than Frank, were still at school. The living room had beautiful white couches that begged you to sit on them, a glass coffee table that (unlike in my house, which while clean obviously looked like a home that had children in it) had not a single smudge. In the kitchen, there was a breakfast table that could've been an exact replica of the one the Tanner family ate at in *Full House*. It was a very inviting home. Frank grabbed an air mattress out of the closet and blew it up in the living room for us to catch a nap before the rest of his family came home. I didn't want to be sleeping when Frank's family came home, but that's exactly what happened.

When Tony walked in, I was in all my bed-head glory (thank goodness I wasn't wearing wigs yet). Tony was shorter than Frank and Michael and rounder, something his brothers loved to remind him of. He seemed nice but reserved. I wasn't used to that. My family treated everyone who came to our home like an old friend. This was odd to me and made me very self-conscious. I was hyper aware of everything I did. Frank and Tony played video games, laughing and talking about people they knew. I felt excluded and isolated, so I took out my phone and just started internet browsing. When I feel out of place, I like to disappear; can't feel out of place if I'm not here.

When his brother went to the bathroom, Frank scooted closer to me and whispered, "It's kind of rude for you to be on your phone."

"What am I supposed to do? You guys were having a conversation that I wasn't a part of."

He smiled and nudged me slightly. "Just jump in."

After his brother returned, I made every effort to "jump in," but everything I did fell flat. After a while, his youngest brother, Michael, came home. He was different—he was friendly and welcoming. I'd hung out with him when he came to stay with Frank for about a month during film school, and he seemed genuinely excited to see me again. I was happy (and relieved) to see him again too. The tallest of the three brothers, he was also very funny, and optimistic. He didn't look like Frank, who was an exact replica of his mom, or Tony (an exact replica of their dad). He had a look of his own. Years later, my daughter Aaliyah would be *his* exact replica. Michael didn't stay long. Like most teens his age, he had a life, and as quick as he had come home, he departed.

I watched the time slowly pass by. We had arrived around noon, and it was now almost six o'clock in the evening. Any moment now, Frank's mom would be coming home from work. I wasn't necessarily afraid, but I *was* apprehensive. After that first encounter on Frank's birthday, where she completely ignored me, my hopes weren't high for the mother-in-law/

daughter-in-law relationship I'd always dreamt of. But this was her house, and I knew that if things went south, I'd have to leave.

About a half hour later, Tony announced that their mom would be home soon. I could see Frank was excited, and through his brother, I found out that I was the first girl he'd ever brought home for any of them to meet. It made me feel special and calmed my nerves a bit. At least there was no bar I had to live up to.

As slow as time had been moving before, it suddenly sped up like it was on crack. Any moment now, Frank's mother would be walking through those doors. Finally, the moment came. Margaret walked in with a huge smile on her face, excited to see Frank. The two were identical, with their matching oval-shaped faces and large slender noses. They both hated their noses, but I thought they were beautiful. They both had large wide brown eyes, and a frame so thin gaining weight seemed impossible.

Frank got up to give her a hug. I stood up too and followed him over to say my greetings. She looked at me, and I can't remember if we hugged or not, but I do remember that it was the last time she acknowledged me until dinner. She had cooked, and her boyfriend had come over. He was an extremely friendly man, who seemed genuinely interested in me, asking questions about my family, and what I went to school for, if I had any siblings, where I was originally from. Having him there definitely made me feel more at ease. He was short, and I could tell he might have been considered handsome once upon a time. He wasn't out of shape, but he also wasn't in the shape I would have imagined after Margaret had raved to Frank about him having been a Taekwondo instructor. He looked as if the only involvement he had with martial arts was as a spectator.

Frank's mom was focused on him, and only him. So was Tony. It was like the only people at the table who knew I was alive were Frank and his mother's boyfriend. I wasn't the girl they'd imagined for Frank, so I was a nuisance. It felt like they wanted me out of the way so that the *real* girlfriend could appear. At some point, he ran out of questions, and I ran out of answers. Everyone had finished eating and was just sitting around chatting, so I took out my phone. I was playing some game when his mother said, "Excuse me. I don't allow phones at the dinner table." I'm not confrontational, at all. But when I heard the tone of her voice, and looked up to see her shooting daggers, I wanted to say something. I wanted to say something smart. I wanted to say something rude. But I didn't. I just smiled and said, "Oh, I'm sorry," and put my phone away. I did, however, shoot a look at Frank, and he knew exactly what it meant. I was angry. No one, other than Frank, has ever really seen me angry. They only got glimpses. It takes a lot to flip that switch, but once it's switched, I go from Larry to Sharon real quick—and anyone who knows my parents knows how day and night the two can be. Frank didn't like me being upset.

"Since when can't we have any phones at the table? This has never been a rule," he spoke up.

His mom slowly looked over at him and said, "I've never liked you guys having your phones at the table."

"Yeah, but you've never told us to put them away."

Frank was talking back to his mother, in defense of me. I noticed it, and she noticed, but poor Frank was just standing up for his girlfriend. I don't think he realized the target he'd placed on my back. A target that would remain until well after our wedding. In fact, it'd last right up until I gave birth to our first child.

10

Married with Children

The visit with Frank's mom and his brothers was pleasant enough. I found myself enjoying Tucson. We left and made our way back to Los Angeles, back to the struggle of life post-graduation. We worked on more short films that paid just enough for us not to starve as we saved to find our own place, and while I should've been focused on gaining stability, I was pushing marriage more than ever. I had met his family, what more did I need to do?

Yeah, I was delusional, but I guess he was too, because one morning during breakfast, he proposed to me. Breakfast was my favorite meal of the day, but not because I thought it was important. Breakfast just offered the best foods. I should've known something was up, because Frank never ate breakfast. He had made my favorite—waffles, bacon, sausage, eggs, and hash browns, plus some fresh-squeezed orange juice.

Frank watched me as I was eating. I wasn't confused by him not making himself a plate. Despite the amount of food,

I knew he didn't like breakfast and just assumed he was doing something nice for me. He asked how I liked my waffles, and after my confirmation that it was delicious, he asked me to stand up. Now I was getting suspicious. He told me he loved me more than he'd ever loved anyone else, and that our experiences together brought him more joy than he ever thought possible. (Note for the readers: We'd had sex by this point and were having it regularly. I'll spare too many details for my siblings, as I *know* they'll read this and I'm sure they've already gagged at the fact that I mentioned us kissing.)

Frank got down on one knee. I started crying before he even hit the ground.

"Will you marry me?"

I cried for a good ten minutes before saying yes. Immediately, I drove to my family home to announce the news to my parents, but it turned out they already knew. Apparently, Frank had asked my dad's permission already, and they were just waiting on my announcement.

I finally felt like I was back on track. For so long, I had felt as if time had frozen for me since leaving Chicago. I was so far behind all my peers that no matter what I did, I could never catch up. But here I was, engaged and about to be married. It had all worked out in the grand scheme of things. I was beyond happy. And for the first time in my life, I felt like it was okay for good things to happen to me (can we say, tragic serenity?).

Unfortunately, my siblings did not feel the same. I found out later that Keke and the twins had a family meeting after hearing the news. They liked Frank, but none of them wanted me getting married and moving out of the house. We had been such a tight unit for so long. The idea of me going off on my own, separate from them, was unheard of. They had to stop it. My parents were happy with Frank, because *I* was happy with Frank. The twins absolutely *adored* him...until he threatened to take me away. Keke knew where this could go from the start; she was older, and as a result more reserved.

Their planning was futile, although I never quite learned what their plan was. Apparently, they'd only had the one meeting to decide they needed a plan. It never got further than that, so the wedding planning was in full swing. It was a fantastic distraction from being unemployed. By now Keke was in her early twenties and had moved out. My parents had moved to a less expensive house, and Keke had moved into her own apartment. My parents helped pay for the wedding, but it was clear they didn't have much money to spare, not like they would have had before, or like they do now for my next wedding (hint hint, Mom and Dad).

I scoured the internet for information on DIY weddings, which honestly turned out to be way more fun than just hiring someone else to plan it. I was involved in every aspect of the wedding and had the time of my life making our centerpieces and other decorations. We had these beautiful white lanterns that we put navy blue candles in to serve as centerpieces. Those were our colors, white and navy blue. We had white and navy blue rose petals to line the aisle, and navy blue roses sprinkled across the white tablecloths during the reception. Navy blue had been my grandmother's favorite color, and since she was no longer alive to see the beautiful woman her shy granddaughter had become, I wanted her memory to be felt.

We lost Grandma Mildred back in 2009, and I don't think I ever truly processed it. Even to this day, the mere thought of her can bring me to tears. You know that people won't be around forever, but you expect them to be, if that makes sense. I remember a few months before her death, we watched Tyler Perry's *Madea Goes to Jail*. She loved Derek Luke. She kept saying, "If I was a young woman, that's the kind of man I'd need." We ate Burger King and laughed at her attraction to this much younger man. It was our last memory together, one I will cherish for the rest of my life.

The wedding planning wasn't very stressful—there were only a few minor hiccups (bridesmaids backing out at the last minute, the officiant backing out at the last minute, forty uninvited out-of-town guests showing up in Los Angeles to attend the wedding at the last minute) that we maneuvered quite well. My bachelorette party was *everything*. Even though my parents had moved to a smaller house, it wasn't exactly what you would call small (in fact, looking back now, it was our favorite), so my mom and Keke decided to throw the party there. They invited all my friends—the few friends I had, Keke's friends who I also knew, and my mom's friends. From the moment everyone walked in, the games began.

You had to choose an X-rated name for yourself as soon as you entered the house. If anyone referred to you by your actual name, they had to take a shot. I can't remember anyone's name (including my own) except for my friend Ron's, which was "Dick Sucking Lips." Ron and I had met at an audition for some singing show years earlier, and although neither of us were called back, we won something even better: friendship. We must've called him "Dick Sucking Lips" a million times that night. Watching my mom's friends say it was the best part. My mom referred to him as Ron *once* and, agreeing to be a team player, took her shot despite not being much of a drinker. She did not make the mistake again.

We had fun all night, but the best part was the stripper, Flash. He stole the show when he sat me in my parents' dining room chair and flipped me *and* the chair completely upside down and back again. I couldn't look at that chair without blushing for weeks after that. I don't think I went to sleep that night. I just kind of passed out on the cold marble floor with whipped cream from Flash's "party games" still all over my breasts.

The next morning, my head was pounding. My mom was rushing through the house making all kinds of noise, telling me I had to get up and get to the hotel to get my hair and makeup started. The wedding was poolside at a nice hotel in Los Angeles. Thank God it was a beautiful day—hot, but beautiful. I made it to the hotel in time to take a shower and rid my body of the previous night's events. I remember being stressed, but I can't remember why, maybe because it was my wedding day? I mean, I was perfectly calm before the lady started on my hair and makeup, but now I was freaking out. My dad was his usual jovial self, making jokes, and literally putting a smile on everybody's face. I remember thinking, "How is he so damn calm?!" Before he walked me down the aisle, he smiled and said, "This is it!" I immediately started crying, and he said, "You should be crying, this is a great day. Happy tears are alright!"

I remember the cake being late, and I remember the room hadn't been set up like it should have been. I also remember both of my parents telling me to relax, because years from now I would barely remember the day because I'd be so busy. They were right. I remember walking down the aisle. I remember Frank and I crying. I remember Keke and her best friend (who was like my little sister), Taylor, crying. I remember singing Selena's "Dreaming of You" to Frank, I remember our first dance being to Journey's "Open Arms." I remember dancing to the "Cha Cha Slide," and then I have nothing else. I don't even remember going to sleep that night. I just remember that we had a brunch the next day to thank everyone for coming, and that only sixty people had RSVPed, but a hundred showed up, so we had to buy extra tables and meals to cover the extra bodies.

So, I was married now. No longer Loreal Chanel Palmer. I was now Mrs. Loreal Chanel Wimberly. I was part of a whole new family, and what did a new family need? Children. If you can't tell, I was playing catch up. But with who? Myself. I had decided years ago that I would complete certain events by certain ages, and in my mind, moving to California had set me back. I had to make up for lost time. I could've just let life unfold, but no. I was trying to meet arbitrary deadlines that I had set for myself; I'm a Capricorn after all.

These early years of marriage I like to refer to as the "dark years." We still had no consistent income, but we were able to make it by moving far from Los Angeles to Moreno Valley. We found a cute and spacious two-bedroom apartment, and we even adopted a blue nose pit bull that we named Lady. She looked scary, but she was the biggest baby and had the cutest relationship with my parents' puggle, Charlie. They were besties.

I was twenty-three creeping up on twenty-four, freshly married, in a new apartment, and in a new city. I don't know if maybe that explains what happened to me next, but I began to feel odd. About a month into our new life, I noticed I wasn't sleeping. I would stay up all night, and I wouldn't feel tired. Then I started having weird thoughts, like I couldn't go to sleep before 2:00 a.m., because if I did, I wouldn't wake up the next morning. So, I'd stay up until 2:00 a.m., go to sleep around then, then wake up at 5:00 a.m. and just start the day like normal.

At a routine check-up, I flagged likely for depression, so my doctor prescribed citalopram. I had felt like this before once, when we had just gotten back from Louisiana, and I got over it. I thought I could again, but if this would help, why not? I didn't think of how I felt as depression, more like being in a funk. I took it for a few weeks, and then things escalated. One night, I woke up in a panic.

"Frank, call an ambulance! I'm having an aneurysm, I know it," I screamed.

"What? You're not making sense?"

"I can't breathe! Feel my chest!"

"What am I looking for?"

"Call them now or I'll die!"

He called 911, and the EMTs drove me to the hospital with him trailing behind in our car. After waiting for hours with me, and the nurses completing their exams, I was given Ativan through an IV and felt miraculously better. They gave me a prescription and told me to follow up with my doctor. When I did, she offered an explanation that I wasn't ready to accept.

"The anxiety started after the citalopram?" She asked.

"No, I was anxious before."

She wrote something down. "But the citalopram made it worse?"

"Much worse."

She wrote something down again. Then she gave me a form to fill out that asked if I ever had experiences of intense highs or extreme lows, if I ever stumbled over my words, had reckless spending habits, or anything like that. After filling out the sheet and returning it to her, she gave me a referral to a psychiatrist.

"Sometimes," she started, "SSRIs can trigger a manic episode in individuals with bipolar disorder."

I stopped listening. Nothing was wrong with me. I took her referral and stuffed it in my glove compartment. I was fine. Only I wasn't. This episode escalated to me hearing someone whispering my name and seeing bugs that weren't there crawling all over me or the walls. I figured it was stress. I had just gone through a huge change in my life. I was still adjusting. So, after the episode passed, I figured I had adjusted and focused on the next phase of my life plan: to have a baby.

I found myself pregnant rather quickly. I was so excited. I wanted to surprise Frank. To make him cupcakes or something that said, "Congratulations, Daddy!" Instead, I found myself running out of the bathroom screaming, with my pee-filled stick sporting a positive sign. He was ecstatic. I had always heard that you should wait until you're twelve weeks to announce a pregnancy. Something about the crucial stage of development being completed by then.

I was glad we had waited because a week later I ended up having a miscarriage. I wasn't too heartbroken. I knew that early miscarriages were far more common than we think. Most people mistake it as a late period. A couple of months later, I was pregnant again. We had no problem getting pregnant—it was the staying pregnant that was hard. This time I waited a little over a week to tell Frank, despite his immense support; I couldn't keep disappointing him. I felt like I'd rather be disappointed by myself. I ended up miscarrying the day after I told him, before my appointment was even scheduled. The third time I found out I was pregnant, I wasn't excited. This time

I was terrified. I don't even remember how I told Frank, but we were both afraid for me to even move. I remember doing everything slowly, as if speed had somehow been the cause of my previous miscarriages. We felt a small sense of relief as we drove to our second appointment for this pregnancy. The first one had only been to draw blood. This time, we'd get to see a heartbeat.

Only, we wouldn't. I cried in the car ride home following my OB's revelation that my HCG levels, the hormones that track a healthy, developing pregnancy, weren't doubling as they were supposed to after forty-eight hours.

"Is something wrong with me? Should I get tested?"

My OB smiled at me, "No, you're twenty-three and perfectly healthy. It's not as easy to get pregnant as people think. You only have about a twenty-five percent chance each month, and your body has a great way of handling pregnancies that wouldn't have been viable."

I tried to be okay with that reasoning, that my body had sensed something was wrong, and that the miscarriages were part of a natural process. But I still felt like it was *me*. How could this happen three times and something not be wrong with me?

A few months later, I found out I was pregnant again. I had been taking my vitamins, eating better, and walking almost daily around the Rose Bowl (daily is a stretch; it was more so on the days we were in town visiting my parents). It was like wedding prep all over again. I wanted to be in the best shape of my life. I was afraid to tell Frank about the positive test. He had gone through those losses just as I had, the constant peeing on a stick only to find a false sense of hope. He was my rock, telling me that we'd have an amazing marriage whether we had kids or not, but I knew he really wanted kids, and I was afraid of what might happen to us if I couldn't give them to him. What would be my worth?

I showed him the test later that day, and he was excited, albeit reserved. We decided not to tell anyone until after our twelve-week scan. Because I'd had three previous losses, we went to a specialist, a perinatologist who informed us they would be doing a 3D scan. For thirty minutes we watched the doctor scan our baby, our son, as he sucked his thumb, massaged his face, and worked on his bicycle crunches. He was perfectly healthy, and extremely active, although I wouldn't feel his first kicks for a few more weeks.

At nineteen weeks, I knew something was off. There's a lot of discharge during pregnancy, but this was a *lot*. That morning, I noticed blood when I went to the bathroom, but it wasn't bleeding like with my previous losses. This was more like blood-tinged mucus. It was exactly like what I'd imagined a mucus plug would look like, based on the mountains of pregnancy books I'd spent the last few months memorizing.

I was only nineteen weeks; I couldn't be losing my mucus plug. I immediately called my doctor's office, despite it being after hours, and was assured it was nothing.

"Pregnancy is gross," the nurse assured me. "This won't be the first awful thing you see. You're perfectly fine."

I didn't feel fine. I felt uneasy about the entire situation, but I'm not a pusher—I'm more of a pushover; a peacemaker. I didn't want to bother her, and that's how I felt, like a bother. She was an expert. If she said it was nothing, then it was nothing. I tried to push the negative thoughts out of my mind, but every time I went to the bathroom, there was a reminder.

Even when the bleeding did stop, the next trip it would be there again, taunting me.

A few days later, Frank surprised me by taking me to Babies R Us to create our shower registry. I didn't want to jinx myself, so I hadn't bothered to look at anything in person before this moment. It was fine now though; I was in the safety zone. We strolled around that store imagining our perfect nursery, for our perfect baby—we had even saved up a few crumbs of perfect baby money. The store associates gave us the grand presentation, handing me a new mother's gift bag, and giving me mommy-to-be snacks.

As I waddled through the store following our presentation, tagging baby bathtubs and different brands of pacifiers, I noticed I was way more winded than usual. I asked Frank to stop for a moment and decided to test the glider we were standing next to by plopping right down into it. The minute I sat down, it felt like my insides were sliding down slowly after me. I felt my baby kick much lower than usual, and I knew something was wrong. I got up and ran to the bathroom; it was far too soon for him to be this low based on everything I had read. I slammed the stall door shut and pulled my pants down, only to be met with more bleeding and more mucus.

I called the doctor again right there from the bathroom, hyperventilating and gasping through tears.

"Mrs. Wimberly, you have to calm down. You're not losing your mucus plug, it's too soon for that. What you're describing is a severe yeast infection. You need to pick up some Monistat, but not the One-Day. Relax, everything is different when you're pregnant. You're fine."

I hung up the phone and wiped my tears away. I needed to get a grip. I was ruining the pregnancy with my constant worrying. I felt like an idiot. I washed my hands and as I walked out of the bathroom, a worried Frank greeted me.

"Are you okay?"

I smiled. "I'm fine."

I wasn't fine. The next evening, we decided to visit my parents. We loved going over and spending time with the twins. I'm over a decade older than them, but we've always been close. Dad made his famous meatloaf, but he had used the wrong crackers. I don't know how, but he had used some crackers that should've been thrown away a year ago. None of us had the heart to tell him that the meatloaf was...off. So when he tasted it for himself and made the discovery, we all erupted into laughter. Laughing a bit too hard, I knew it was time to go to the bathroom.

As soon as I sat on the toilet, I felt like something was coming out of me.

"Frank!" I screamed. He was there before I even finished screaming.

I asked him, begged him, to look. Something was happening. He looked between my legs, and his face was a mix of horror and confusion.

"Something's in there, but I..."

That was it. I was going to the doctor, and I was going to force my OB to tell me what the hell was happening. I had no pain whatsoever, but *something* was coming out. I wasn't crazy. I *felt* it, and Frank had *seen* it.

I showed up at my doctor's office unannounced and demanded to be seen by my OB. The nurses kept smiling and trying to calm me down, offering me water and asking how I felt. I feel fucking mad! I didn't say that, of course, but my face showed it. They stopped bothering me, leaving me alone until it was finally my turn to see the doctor. She took me into one of the open rooms, visibly bothered, but agreeing to examine me—I didn't really give her a choice. She was short with me, skipping the formalities; she wanted to get me out of there as soon as possible despite putting on her best face to show otherwise.

"Okay, Mrs. Wimberly, you are worried, and everything is fine, so let me just show you, okay?"

She displayed a painful smile as I placed my legs into the stirrups waiting for her to place the speculum. When she finally did look through it, her face went white. She stood up immediately and walked over to the counter.

She didn't look at us as she spoke. "Your membranes are bulging. You can't continue this pregnancy."

Time literally froze as she explained everything to Frank. I must have blocked it all out, because I don't remember hearing what was wrong from her. I was told to rush to the hospital immediately. I remember sitting in the passenger seat as Frank told me it would all be okay.

"How? How is it gonna be okay? I have to give birth now! He can't survive!"

I hit the dashboard as hard as I could, bruising my hands in the process, but I didn't care. I cried and he cried with me. Then our tears turned into something else: hope. Maybe she was wrong? What if we had caught it in time, and here at the hospital they could save him?

We arrived at the hospital and were greeted by the sympathetic smiles of nurses. The doctor had told them to expect us, and they knew—they knew we wouldn't be leaving with a baby. An older nurse wheeled me into a private room. It was the labor and delivery room, so it was set up with everything a new mother would need. There was a fancy neonatal scale that they would use to check a newborn's weight and a bassinet for the new baby to sleep in. The nurse caught me looking at the items and scolded the other nurse who was waiting in the room.

"I told you this couldn't be in here. Get it out now."

The nurse scrambled to remove the items as the older nurse smiled at me. I met her eyes, but I couldn't smile back. I guess I had forgotten how.

After removing the "forbidden items," the nurse returned and helped me undress; I guess I had forgotten how to do that too. After they played dress-up with me and treated me like a starved, lost puppy, they placed me in the Trendelenburg position, with my head tilted towards the floor and my feet pointing towards the ceiling, so that they could scan my baby. Frank watched and smiled as our son came onto the screen, sucking his thumb as usual, but I couldn't look. Why should I look? He wouldn't be there much longer. He wouldn't even exist much longer.

My entire family came there to rally behind me. They rushed in one by one, a mix of concern and condolences. Keke demanded second opinions, demanded to know what could be done.

"Y'all have to do something. This isn't making any sense to me. How can the doctors do nothing?"

I appreciated her, but the words stung. There *was* nothing they could do; that had been made clear. My amniotic fluid was tinged green by meconium due to the shock the baby had experienced from the constant sliding motions over the past few days. I discovered, at some point, that I had something called an incompetent cervix, and while there was a workaround called a cerclage that would enable me to successfully carry children in the future, it wouldn't save this one. I'd have to let him go. I'd have to let him go because something *was* wrong with me after all. I was *incompetent*. My inability to stand up for myself, and him, when I *knew* something was wrong had caused him stress, which led to the meconium; now I was being told that even if they did try to prolong the pregnancy by placing an emergency cerclage, or even leaving me in Trendelenburg until viability, the chances were not good.

The doctor came in and explained how the night would go. I would be given medication to ripen my cervix and induce contractions. It's the same medication they use for medical abortions. That's what they were calling this, a medical abortion. Shortly after that, they administered the medication, and all I could do at that point was wait.

"It won't be long. He's very tiny so we won't need to wait until ten centimeters," the nurse explained as she administered the medication and adjusted the machines they had hooked me up to.

My dad tried to lighten the mood in a way that only he could. If it had been anyone else, I probably would've been upset, but he had a way of making people feel like things weren't that bad...even though I knew they were. Keke didn't know what to say, so she just kept reminding me that she was here and loved me. My mom was simply *there* for me. I think I appreciated that most. She knew that nothing she could do would fix this, but she wanted me to know that I was far from alone.

As I lay there in the hospital bed, hooked up to the beeping and whooshing monitors that revealed a perfectly healthy baby, and a perfectly healthy mom, I didn't understand why

I couldn't keep him. I mean, I could comprehend what was happening, but I couldn't, or wouldn't wrap my head around the situation. He was mine, and I *wanted* him, so bad. What had I done to deserve this? What could I have done to prevent this? I had always believed that everything in life happened for a reason. What was the reason here? What action had I committed in the past that resulted in this painful punishment?

Keke left around midnight, after telling me she loved me and it would be okay eventually. My dad followed not too long after, kissing both Frank and I on the foreheads and telling us that he loved us. My mom stayed, watching over me silently. I could tell she didn't know what to say, and I honestly don't know what I would've wanted to hear. *It'll all be over soon. You can try again. I love you.* These were things I already knew, but what good would they have done? Sometimes silence is the best medicine.

With just Frank and my mom left in the room, I started having contractions. I remember feeling a mix of excitement and horror. I'd waited so long to experience this moment, but this wasn't how I wanted to experience it. I wanted to come home with a baby, but that wasn't going to happen. As the contractions came sooner, I prepared as any woman in labor would. I breathed through each round as the intensity increased. Frank held my hand and my mom counted for me. Everyone kept telling me how strong I was. I had no choice.

I was asked if I wanted an epidural, which I fiercely refused. I had planned to have my baby naturally, and if I could do nothing else for him, I wanted to feel his entry into this world, no matter how short his time here would be. No one questioned me, but I could tell they thought I was foolish. Why go through all this pain for a baby that I wouldn't take home? I didn't care. He lived inside of me. I felt him move; I talked to him. I was determined to experience this final moment with him—his final moments.

Around 2:00 a.m., a nurse came in, announcing it was time to push. The hospital room became a madhouse within minutes. Nurses were rushing in and out prepping for delivery. My mom, for the first time all night, stood up and began gathering her things.

"You and Frank take this moment to say goodbye alone. I don't need to be here. I know it doesn't feel like it now, but you *will* be okay."

She kissed me on my forehead and turned to Frank to do the same. Then she left. Frank held my hand with tears in his eyes as the nurse told me it was okay to start pushing when I felt a contraction. This moment that should have been filled with excitement had me in a strange state. I can't explain it. I knew that once I pushed, that was it. It would all be over, and I could start to move on. Could I move on? I pushed three times, and he was out. I had a cousin who'd gone through something similar. She had warned me not to look at him. It would be harder if I looked. I didn't look, but I cried as Frank did.

He looked at our baby and told me that he looked like me. He touched him, and he told him he loved him. That *we* loved him. I felt ashamed that I couldn't look at him. After all, it was my incompetence that had cut his life so extremely short. A sweet nurse came in with a little blue blanket, and she wrapped him up. I turned my head and held my eyes shut tightly. I didn't want to see anything that I couldn't unsee. Later that same nurse came back in with photos of my baby she had taken for me.

"You might want to look at him later."

In the photos, I would see later that she had dressed him up, pinning the hat and onesie strategically so that the material wouldn't all swallow his tiny body. She crafted a memory book, consisting of several posed photos, the blanket and hat he had been in, as well as his footprints. He came into this world at nineteen weeks and six days, one day too soon for him to be issued a birth certificate, so she had made me one and put that in there as well.

I moved slowly the next morning. I didn't want to go home. The longer I stayed at the hospital, the longer I could avoid facing the world, facing the hordes of nosey relatives who would want to hear what happened, the family friends who wanted to tell me what their sister's boyfriend's wife had done when she had gone home after going through something similar.

I went home to my parents' house after being discharged from the hospital. They were babysitting the five-year-old son of a family friend. Within seconds he greeted me.

"Sorry about your baby," he said.

I nodded and offered what I hoped resembled a smile before heading up to the bedroom that had belonged to the twins. I would be staying there while I dealt with this. While I dealt with all the issues any new mother deals with—fluctuating hormones, soreness, and lactation—except I didn't have a baby to feed or hold or rock to sleep. I was depressed, and every time someone assured me I could try again, I just wanted to yell, "I don't want *another* baby. I want *my* baby."

11

One Day at a Time

My anxiety was in overdrive after the loss. I made at least five trips to the ER in the next month, convinced I was having a heart attack. I know now that these were panic attacks, but at the time I genuinely thought I was on my way off the Earth. Frank stopped being concerned, no longer accompanying me on these trips, but waiting at home for my return the next morning. I still wanted a baby, but I knew my body needed to recover.

I started doing research on an incompetent cervix. I learned that there was something called a transvaginal cerclage, and a transabdominal cerclage—one went in through the vagina, the other through the abdomen and was like a C-section procedure. The transabdominal cerclage was stronger, so I wanted that one. I found multiple experts who were all more sympathetic than my OB had been. The consensus was that I should get it done either before pregnancy, or before ten weeks of pregnancy. I wanted it done yesterday.

It wasn't covered by my insurance, so I had to let the idea go for now. Frank and I had booked jobs on a horror short based on the *Resident Evil* franchise that we were really excited about. I was hired as a production designer, and this provided great distraction. I was finally working on a film that belonged to the genre I had hoped to create. Things were looking up. We shortly found ourselves working on a pilot starring Raven-Symoné, and by this point I was feeling better.

All good things, however, must come to an end, and in October of 2013 we found ourselves unemployed, which stretched into the better part of the next year. The freelance nature of the industry was getting real old, real fast. We moved to a smaller apartment to make what little money we had saved last longer, but even then, we were on borrowed time. Frank was on the phone one evening with his mom, telling her how things honestly were. She suggested we move to Tucson. It was cheaper, and we could stay with her while we got our shit together. At this time, my parents had moved to an even smaller house down the street from the Rose Bowl. My parents were never extravagant people, so with Keke and me gone, they had wanted something smaller with no stairs, similar to how they would've lived back in Illinois. Living with them was not a comfortable option. With nowhere else to turn, we packed up our 2001 Chevy Cavalier and made the move from LA to Arizona.

I was nervous about staying with Frank's mom, but I kept telling myself it wouldn't be for long, that we would be in our own place soon. Something about a long drive has always calmed me. Somewhere along the border between California and Arizona, we stopped at a gas station next to a Popeye's.

We had dinner, and for one moment things felt okay. Almost like we had wanted this move, or that we had planned it.

That feeling faded by the time we got to Frank's mom's house. I immediately felt out of place. I just wanted to go home, but I didn't have one to go to anymore. I started writing again: music, movies, and film ideas. While Frank was out on job interviews, I'd be on my laptop creating imaginary worlds about the life I wished I was living. It wasn't all bad. I learned to deal with his mother's presence quite well, even though I felt that she didn't want me for her son.

During the days where we were alone, Frank and I would try to find time to be intimate. Usually in the shower. One day when we thought we were alone in the house, we found out we actually weren't. We walked out of the shower to find the back door to the duplex wide open. I thought we were being robbed. Frank walked out to find his brother sitting on the patio furniture. I stayed in the living room, but I heard him ask, "What's up?" His brother's response mortified me.

"I get that you guys are married adults and all, but she's really loud."

Was I really loud? How did I sound? Was I annoying?

Later that night, his mom talked to him about respecting people's houses. Again, mortified. I wanted to crawl away and hide. No one ever said anything directly to me, so I behaved normally. But I felt as though his mom was looking through me instead of at me, and I didn't want to show her any weakness. I wasn't a confident person, but around her I pretended to be. I refused to appear weak in front of someone I thought would use it against me.

Time went on, and Frank and I were more careful—or were we? I was on birth control, yet somehow shortly after

Christmas, about three months after we had arrived, I found myself pregnant again. I wasn't happy. Not at first. This wasn't the situation I wanted to welcome a baby to. I decided to wait before telling Frank. I had just received this huge royalty back payment from some songs I'd written, and we were talking about getting a place once he had secured a permanent job. In the end, I didn't actually tell him; he found out. I guess I wasn't hiding it well, what with my morning sickness and sleeping all day.

He was far more excited than I had been, and he made me feel a lot better about it. What *really* made me feel better was when he told me a few days later that he'd been offered a permanent position at a local crafts store that had previously only been seasonal. It wasn't great pay, but in Tucson we'd be fine. More than fine. We started looking at apartments, and despite our efforts to keep things quiet, it was a small house that was full of people. His mom found out I was pregnant before we could tell her.

She was excited about her grandchild and wanted us to stay. Just until the baby came, so that she could help me. We were all on edge after the loss when it came to this pregnancy, so nobody wanted me to do anything, especially once I got the cerclage at around twelve weeks. So, we agreed to stay. She wasn't charging us rent, so we would be able to save up quite a bit.

The pregnancy went smoothly during the first three months. On the day of my cerclage appointment, I was a ball of nerves. They performed it at twelve weeks, before the baby weighed much of anything, before the cervix started to open due to the pressure of said weight. I would need a spinal epidural, and then they would go inside vaginally and literally stitch my cervix closed. Depending on how "weak" my cervix was, this cerclage should be strong enough to support the pregnancy. That *should* made me nervous.

I came in at 6:00 a.m. for an 8:00 a.m. procedure. As luck would have it, there were three emergency C-sections that day, so I wasn't even seen until maybe eight or nine that night. By the time the nurse came in to take me back for the epidural, I was over it—or so I thought. I had never had any type of surgery before, and getting a spinal made me way more nervous than I wanted to admit. I had this fear of being paralyzed or getting one of those horrible spinal headaches I had read about. Or worse, I had read about this horrible mishap where this lady had somehow caught meningitis due to some type of contamination during her spinal. I voiced this concern to my doctor, who laughed it off and asked, "Was this in the South?"

You have to be completely still for a spinal epidural, but I was shaking uncontrollably, and to my surprise, tears started flowing. My teeth were chattering so loudly that about three nurses cradled around me like I was a sick infant, cooing and reassuring me that it would be okay. I finally calmed down enough for them to give me the spinal. Immediately, I felt a rush of heat take over my lower half.

"Is it supposed to feel like this?" I asked.

"What do you feel?" The nurse responded.

My team was extraordinary to say the least. After describing what I felt, she assured me that it was normal. I lay there until the medicine had taken full effect. Then they lifted me to another bed that they wheeled down to the OR. Once there, they started scrubbing me down and using iodine. I tried to look down to see what they were doing, but with my lower half out of commission, my movements were limited. Instead, I turned to talk to the anesthesiologist. He was funny and cracked jokes to lighten the mood. I only freaked out once when I felt the paralysis creeping up towards my chest. He adjusted some stuff on his end and propped me up a bit more—the feeling moved back down.

It took about thirty minutes to place the cerclage, but it was hours before I could go home. I had to meet two conditions before I could be discharged: I had to be able to walk by myself, and I had to be able to pee by myself. They said I should be able to walk in about an hour. It took a little over two. Peeing took longer. By the time I did, they were relieved. My bladder had been dangerously full. It was well after midnight when we finally left the hospital, and all I really wanted to do was stop by McDonald's and get a sausage McGriddle. Frank stopped and got me *two*.

The rest of my pregnancy was relatively uneventful. I saw the perinatologist every two weeks and found out we were having a boy. I don't think my nerves truly calmed until I was at twenty-eight weeks. Babies born after this point in the pregnancy do really well in the Neonatal Intensive Care Unit, or NICU. Once he had passed that marker, I let my family throw me a baby shower. It would be back home in Pasadena, and this time Frank and I would take the train. We booked a private room, and I slept the whole way, damn near—I woke up for all the free meals that were included, of course.

The baby shower was everything I could've dreamt it would be. My mom and one of her good friends, Carlita, planned it. Chef Larry was in charge of the menu, and there were no leftovers. There were even some items that I hadn't gotten the chance to taste. Although I did have a cupcake or two, or three. It was nice being home with my family, but I couldn't wait to get back to Tucson. I was thirty-three weeks pregnant during the shower, and I was carrying low. I spent most of my waking moments exhausted.

About two weeks later, I ended up being induced. We arrived at the hospital around 7:00 p.m., and by 11:00 p.m. I was begging for an epidural. I just *knew* I was nine centimeters, and the fact that all this pain was happening at only five centimeters confirmed that I did not want to do this naturally. Epidural, please! Immediately after the epidural had been administered, I was out cold. I didn't wake up again until the pain woke me up. I pushed the button and asked for more, but the nurse who checked me said it was time to push—there would be no more epidural.

In about five big pushes, my son entered the world screaming. I cried. Frank cried. The baby cried. My son was born July 19, 2014, at 4:58 a.m., and he was beautiful. We named him Alexander, after *Superman*'s Lex Luthor. He was only five pounds, fourteen ounces. Extremely tiny, but he was perfect. I took to motherhood instantaneously, staying up most of the night just watching him breathe.

Parenthood was easy with nurses all around, but when we got him home, it was just us. That first week was torture, as he cried all hours of the day and night. Frank and I started crying with him, begging for him to please just go to sleep. We would sleep in shifts, but even during my sleep shift I'd have to get up, as we had decided to breastfeed him. I was losing sleep, and this triggered the same scenario as the last time I'd been that sleep-deprived.

I didn't have crazy thoughts this time, just horrible depression. I thought maybe it was hormones at first, but as the weeks went by, I found myself more and more withdrawn. I loved my baby, but I had no energy. I felt hollow. Eventually, I started thinking that I was a horrible mother, and that my son would be better off without me. I was a failure in every sense of the word. I couldn't even give him life without help.

One morning, as I was showering, I collapsed. I hit the ground and started crying, but I didn't know why. Frank had heard me fall, and he came running.

"Did you fall?"

I looked up. "No."

He started to help me up, but I stopped him, finally telling him how depressed and empty I had been feeling. That I felt like I wanted to die. I couldn't look at him as I spoke.

"I need help."

He got me out of the shower and dressed me, all while our son was asleep in his crib. Then Frank carried him, still sleeping, out to the car and strapped him into the car seat. That quickly, he had found an in-patient mental health center that took our insurance and would see me without an appointment. I agreed to go, because I knew something was wrong, but that agreement was temporary. When I was checked in and given a room after intake, I *knew* I didn't belong here. I freaked out and demanded to be released. I was there of my own free will, after all.

Only my behavior was erratic at best, and they refused to let me leave. I threatened them. I called the police, who never came. And then, when none of that worked, I cried. I went to my "room" and I screamed. *Why did I come here? What the hell is wrong with me?* The one time I asked for help, instead of suffering in silence, *this* was where it led me. I wasn't ready to give up and demanded to see someone, *anyone*, with the authority to have me released this very moment. The charge nurse gave me an Ativan and told me that no one would be able to see me until tomorrow, and that I could go home then. I took the Ativan, went back to my room, and I cried until I fell asleep.

The next morning, I was prepared to leave. I would see the doctor at 10:30, then I would be released. I was up at 8:00 a.m., showered, and then grabbed a book from the small library they had at the facility. It was a book called *Buster Midnight's Cafe*. I had never heard of it, but it captivated me. It made me feel like I wasn't in a mental health facility, like I was back in my room at home, and everything was okay. At nine o'clock they called us for breakfast. I brought the book with me to the small cafeteria as I ate reheated frozen pancakes and sausages, and then went back to the library to read my book.

A nice nurse came by and announced that group would begin at 11:30. I would be gone by then, I thought. The doctor saw me early, at 10:15. I had learned the day before that hysterics would get me nowhere, so I was calm, cool, and collected as I explained there had been a mistake. That I was going through a tough time after having a baby, that my hormones were raging, and I had come here because the intensity of my emotions had frightened me. She listened carefully, nodding here and *mhm*-ing there. Finally, she spoke.

"When you came in yesterday, you gave us permission to access your medical records. I received them this morning, and it says that you likely have bipolar disorder. Are you medicated?"

I shook my head no.

"These episodes will keep happening. They're spaced out now, but eventually they will be closer together. It will become very hard for you to function normally without medication. Do you understand?"

I nodded yes. Anything to get out of there.

"Then you understand I can't let you leave until I get you on a proper medication regimen. You're a risk to yourself and potentially others."

What others? I would never hurt my baby, or Frank. I felt insulted. The cool was gone, and I was ready to flip.

"You can't keep me here. Nothing is wrong with me."

"You told our nurses that you were suicidal."

"No, I told them that I sometimes wished I would disappear."

"As in death."

"No, as in disappear."

We were getting nowhere. She explained to me that my questionnaire and my reaction to the SSRI had strongly suggested bipolar disorder. That's the closest they could get to a definitive diagnosis: a *strong* suspicion. It became clear to me that I wasn't leaving anytime soon. She explained that my lack of sleep had sent me into an episode, not postpartum hormones. She told me that I wouldn't get better until I had accepted the diagnosis and stuck to my treatment. I said I would. Anything to get out of there.

I ended up going to group after all, and it wasn't so bad. In fact, I went to all the little group sessions and activities they had scheduled for me that day. Art therapy, poetry, some outdoor yoga. I also took the medicine that I was prescribed. The doctor wanted to watch me for three weeks. Instead of fighting, I gave in. She said that I needed a routine, so I created one. Every morning I'd wake up, shower, read my book, and go to breakfast. Then I'd read my book, meet with the doctor, and go to group to share my feelings. I was honest—I told them I didn't think anything was wrong with me, that I sometimes got emotionally overwhelmed, and this time it was just too much to handle. Then I'd go to lunch, art, poetry, read some more, and then eat dinner. After that, I'd read until it was time to go to bed.

On visiting day, Frank brought Alexander. I felt embarrassed—he was bringing my son to see me in a cold visiting room at a mental hospital. I got to hold my baby and feed him. He was on formula now for obvious reasons. Frank seemed angry with me, which only made me more embarrassed. He had told me that he was staying with his mom, because he needed help. I understood, but wondered where that would leave me. He seemed less angry by the end of the visit, but he didn't kiss me goodbye. I figured it was because I was crazy. They had told him I was bipolar and needed medication. Stupid me, I had given them permission to discuss everything with him.

Later that evening was movie night; every Friday was movie night. After dinner, they passed out microwave popcorn and homemade Rice Krispie treats. We all sat together and watched *Back to the Future*, one of my favorite movies. After it was over, I decided to go back to my room and write in the journal they had given me. I asked myself if I really was crazy. I asked myself where my life had gone wrong. Most importantly, I asked myself if my life would ever be right again. If Grandma Mildred had been there, she would've told me the same thing she told all of the other family members who had gone through something that seemed impossible to come back from: keep living. It'll get better.

And it would. When my three-week sentence was up, they sent me home. My follow-ups were scheduled all the way up to six months out. Frank seemed happy but reserved as we drove back to his mom's house. AJ (we were calling the baby AJ now, for Alexander Jacob) was three months now, and he had gotten so big. I felt guilty for the weeks of his life I had missed. I knew he wouldn't remember it, but I would never forget. When we got to Frank's mom's house, she didn't say hi. She just grabbed up AJ and went about the "routine" she had created. I wanted to be angry, but I was also grateful that someone had been there for Frank and AJ.

I was given a new medication when I left the facility, and this one made me extremely spacey and tired. I didn't do much during the day, just colored in these mindfulness coloring books and slept. I wanted to be more present for my baby, so I talked to the doctor at my first outpatient appointment about the side effects. I was going to take them seriously, and stick to the medication, but it couldn't be *this* medication. She switched it to something else, and slowly but surely, I felt myself going back to normal. I started doing more around the house, started taking care of my baby.

By the time AJ was seven months old, I had started at a job in customer service at Verizon Wireless that I loved. Frank switched his hours, so that one of us would always be home. We moved into an apartment building literally right next door to his mom's place. I made friends at work, and on the weekends we would go to downtown Tucson and behave like young people did—except I wasn't drinking any alcohol because I was serious about my medication and it was a no-no to drink while on them. I was still going to my appointments, and my therapist had given me a bipolar disorder workbook.

Every night after putting AJ to bed, I would do a page of the workbook.

My family had heard about my hospitalization, and they blamed Frank. None of this had happened before him. Only, it had. Looking back, I was able to identify that during that period when I stopped going to school, I had likely been in a manic episode. I blew everything off without reason, I was spending and behaving recklessly. But they didn't see it that way. To them, all of my problems had started when I met Frank—I knew that wasn't the case. I was slowly starting to accept my diagnosis. I talked to my parents very infrequently back then. Usually just to catch them up on AJ.

Keke had started working again, and while she and my mom were off traveling somewhere, my dad and the twins came to visit us for Thanksgiving. It was a great visit. My dad came over and cooked dinner. We all ate together—including Frank's family—and watched his favorite movie, *It's a Wonderful Life*. I was sad to see them go, and I had to work their last day. I told myself I would start going to see them more often. I was no longer ashamed of who I was; I was once their perfect daughter, who everyone in my family had seen as perfect, sweet, and destined for greatness, due to my ability to weave a tale out of thin air and read multiple books in a day, or at least that's what they would tell others. I never felt it. I felt like that was the image I was supposed to attain, and if I couldn't, who was I? For a long time, I thought of myself as a failure. Not anymore though. I had finally begun the process of finding myself; at least that's what I thought.

At the beginning of 2015, I found myself pregnant again, this time with a girl. I had a difficult decision to make. My medication was dangerous to an unborn fetus. I could risk it, I could get an abortion, or I could go off the medication during the pregnancy and while breastfeeding. I decided that I would go off the medication. As long as I was still seeing my therapist and doing my workbook, I thought I would be okay. If they noticed anything, then we could reconsider.

Everything was fine—until it wasn't. I started experiencing severe pains while walking. My hips would painfully grind any time I tried to move. I found out that this happens to some women after back-to-back pregnancies. Ain't I lucky? I hadn't worked long enough to receive FMLA, so I was forced to leave my job; again unemployed. Frank's hours had been reduced, and my loss hit us hard. My parents wanted me home, so they could watch over me. Frank was itching to get back to Los Angeles and give working in film another try, so we packed up and went to live with my parents.

Their new place was small, but it felt like home. I was worried my parents would treat Frank differently, and while they weren't exactly thrilled with him, we all got along. This pregnancy was doing a number on my body. Around thirty-two weeks, I was in so much pain, Frank bought a wheelchair for me to get around. I had my cerclage removed at thirty-six weeks and started counting down the seconds until I went into labor. I didn't have to count too long.

My doctor had decided that due to my elevated blood pressure during pregnancy, they would induce at thirty-nine weeks if she didn't come on her own. A week before my scheduled induction, Alexandra Dyan decided she was ready to meet us. At five pounds, two ounces, she was tiny. She was the perfect baby. She slept through the night, which frightened us initially. She didn't cry much and seemed content with just being in my arms. AJ adored her, and at only fourteen months apart, I loved that neither would ever remember a time without the other.

We had found a place before Alexandra (Ali) was born, but we couldn't move in until after she was born. Wanting to save as much as we could, we moved far out again, about an hour away from my parents. That didn't stop us from making long weekend visits. They even visited us once. We were happy with our new little addition to our family. We were living in the middle of nowhere, and once Ali could walk, Auntie Keke (who was busy with work again) bought the kids little motorized cars they could drive. AJ had a Range Rover, and Ali had a pink Hello Kitty Beetle. My extended family was not too fond of our little home in the desert, but we loved it. We'd let the kids drive in the dirt for hours, then we'd come in and make dinner as a family.

After the kids were tucked into bed, Frank and I would binge-watch *Hannibal* or MTV's *Teen Wolf* in between seasons of *American Horror Story*. I missed being close to my extended family, but we were so genuinely happy that I didn't mind it too much. I loved being home with my kids. I loved waking up to their little kisses and having conversations about nothing. They always had so much to say with the few words they knew.

Just before Ali turned two, both kids went through some sort of sleep regression. Frank and I would alternate being up with them, well into the morning. I hadn't restarted my medicine, because I had forgotten anything was wrong with me. Or maybe that's just what I told myself. After about a month of this, I noticed I was depressed. I felt the same way I had in Tucson and thought maybe I just needed a reset. Only this wasn't Tucson. I went to the ER to see about an emergency refill. My prescriptions were old, but I figured they might be able to help anyway. They took me to the psych ward after I uttered the magic words: *I feel like I just wanna disappear.*

I don't remember much about this facility, because immediately I was taken into a room and given Haldol, a powerful antipsychotic, and some other stuff. I was hysterical. I didn't want to go to a psych ward. I just wanted to refill my medication. But that's the problem with mental health. There's a stigma, and because my file had bipolar disorder in it, I was deemed a danger to myself. I obviously didn't want to die, because I was there—I was asking for help.

It didn't matter. The next thing I knew, I was so doped up I couldn't give an accurate depiction of my time there because those memories were unable to accurately form. I only remember flashes. I remember sharing a room with a girl who couldn't talk. She would just grunt. I remember wearing a hideous light blue uniform while eating in a cafeteria that looked like the one from HBO's Oz. I remember my parents coming to bring me clothes so that I didn't have to wear the uniform. I remember a girl and a guy were caught having sex, so she was moved. I remember raging the night after they told me that I needed to stay for five more days because I was suicidal. I raged so bad I started scratching the skin off my wrists. They strapped me down and gave me more Haldol and other medications I was never told the names of. I remember staying strapped in that room until I woke up the next morning and was allowed to shower. I remember an Indian girl was in there with me, who was also bipolar, and she gave me a book on mindfulness. I still have it.

It's all faint, and in chunks, but eventually I was able to leave. They gave me a prescription for some medication that had to be injected once a week. I took a taxi to my parents' new house. It was closer to the hospital, and I don't think Frank was ready to see me yet. I know I wasn't ready to see him. My parents tried to act normal, but whatever they gave me had me out of it. I don't remember anything. According to the twins, I was a zombie. I came home and apparently just sat there.

One night, my mom had plans to meet a friend for dinner at a restaurant, and she invited me to come with her. I guess I said yes, because the twins told me later that I sat at the table with them and was eating slowly and drooling. My mom insisted they were lying, which the twins were known to do. They would often come up with a prank and both go with it. They seemed serious about this, but I have no way of knowing for sure. Like I said, those memories never really formed.

I don't remember how long I stayed with my parents, but eventually Frank came to collect me. His mom had flown in from Tucson to help with the kids, and she wanted to stay with us while I adjusted to my medication. I didn't care. I just wanted to be back home with my babies. They were so happy to see me, and right then and there I vowed to stay on my medication, to be there for them always. They deserved that.

We finished off that year in peace. Things were back to normal. I was back to normal. But work was still spotty at best. Keke was dedicating her time to recording music, and one day while we were all swimming at my parents' house, she announced she was moving to Atlanta to focus on her music career. She asked if Frank and I wanted to come too. Neither of us were sure, so we told her we'd think about it. On the drive home, Frank said he didn't want to move. He had finally met some people who he had hoped would lead to more consistent work. I was ambivalent, and fine with not going.

The next day I spoke with my mom about it. She understood Frank's point, but she knew there was film work in Atlanta too. Plus, the cost of living was significantly lower. I thought about it before presenting her perspective to Frank. We had a long discussion that went on for about two days before finally coming to a decision. I texted Keke that we were moving with her to Atlanta.

She responded with one word: *Thrilled!*

12

The Good Wife

I wish I could say that once we moved to Atlanta, everything was great and Frank and I lived happily ever after, but that would only be partially true. Things *were* great...at first. We moved in with Keke for the first two years in Atlanta; we were both in a transition period and wanted to do it together. Frank quickly found a job he loved, so we were able to contribute financially. The house was huge, and we rarely saw her that first year. She was filming the TV series *Berlin Station* in Germany, then went right into filming season three of *Scream* for MTV. Near the end of that first year, I found myself pregnant again. We were five years into our marriage at this point and weren't really having sex like we used to, so we were quite shocked.

This third pregnancy was extremely difficult; I had hyperemesis gravidarum, which was basically severe morning sickness that lasted the entire pregnancy. By my ninth month, I was surviving on Ensure. I was hospitalized in the final weeks of the pregnancy, sipping broth and hooked up to an IV. Frank was basically raising the kids by himself. They would come to the hospital and spend evenings with me, and I'd hide my tears as I hugged and kissed them goodbye. When my medical team finally made the decision to induce, Frank took the kids to stay with a cousin he had in Atlanta, so that he could be with me.

My labors had been notoriously fast, but this one was not following suit. I was induced at nine in the morning, but we didn't even start pushing until after 10:30 p.m. Aaliyah Sierra Keyana came into the world screaming on April 17 at 11:00 p.m. Named after the late singer, Keke, and my baby sister, Lawrencia Sierra. Despite my inability to keep food down, she was my heaviest baby at six pounds even. They let me hold her as I passed the placenta, and she was beautiful. About thirty minutes later, they had me stand up to get into the wheel-chair to be transferred to the new mothers' ward. That's when I knew something was wrong.

Delivery is messy, but when I stood up, blood was gushing out of me. Frank made a comment, something to the effect of "that's a lot of blood," to which the nurse simply responded, "Yeah." They placed a towel on the wheelchair before I sat down. By the time we reached the maternity floor the towel was completely red. Frank helped me into the bed, and I immediately started shivering. I was told it was the medi-cation they'd given me, so I tried to calm down. This weird feeling came over me. I felt weak. Suddenly, I couldn't hear anything but a whooshing sound. Then I wanted to stand up, so I did. More blood started gushing out. The nurse on this floor agreed with Frank: it was a lot of blood.

She asked me to lie back down while she got the doctor, but I had to use the bathroom, so I got back up. Frank watched me from a chair in the corner of the room as he held Aaliyah.

"Please sit down, Lori. They don't want you walking."

I don't know why I didn't listen, but when I sat on the toilet and saw all the blood just flowing out of me, I panicked. I stood up quickly and tried to make it back to the bed. The next thing I remember, I was on the floor, and Frank and another nurse were trying to pick me up. They got me back into the bed, and the doctor on call came in to examine me. She took one look at all the blood and left the room. I heard someone call some type of code over the hospital intercom, and then a team of doctors and nurses came rushing in. I don't want to get too graphic, so I'll summarize. A clot had stopped my uterus from contracting properly after birth, so I was losing a lot of blood and almost died.

I didn't die. I was weak and had to take tons of supplements, but I got to go home after three days, which was a win for me. Aaliyah met her brother and sister, who were in love instantly. I took to new motherhood like a pro. These were some of the happiest times of my life. I was a stay-at-home mom. Frank came home from work to a warm meal and a spotless house. When Aaliyah was about six months old, I even got on a plane with Frank to visit Keke in Budapest, while she was filming the second season of *Berlin Station*. It felt like the honeymoon we never had, but there was no sex—not for my lack of trying.

It was the same a year later. We had moved into our own two-story, four-bedroom home by then, and Keke was hosting a music festival in Cancún. Frank and I joined her at an all-expenses-paid resort. We woke up every morning around noon and went straight to the beach to drink piña coladas and read.

Then we'd meet Keke after she was done working and get drunk in the pool. Then we'd nap and do the same thing at dinner. I was always in the mood, and Frank was always tired. I started to think something was wrong with me. I'd had the kids relatively back-to-back without really losing the weight I'd gained. I was the heaviest I'd ever been. Maybe he no longer found me attractive.

I knew Frank was bisexual; he'd told me this after we'd had AJ. We were in our bedroom, bored, playing a favorite game of mine—emphasis on *mine*—in which I would force him to respond to ridiculous scenarios, such as: "What would you do if you woke up and your nose was missing?" His response was usually something like, "That would never happen, so I don't have an answer." After an unsuccessful back and forth, I suggested we play truth or dare.

"Truth."

Of course, he chose truth—which was fine, because I hadn't thought of a dare. "Is there anything about you that you've never told me," I asked, expecting some tame childhood story about stealing a candy bar from the grocery store. We all have those, right? Frank hesitated, not long, but it was long enough.

"What is it? Tell me." Being the good, pushy wife that I was, I sat up in the bed and pressed him further. What was it about him that I wouldn't know after all this time? He smiled and assured me that there was nothing. So, I pressed on, and on, and on, and that was when he sat up and looked away from me. He was becoming so irritated with my pushing that I started to play every possible worst-case scenario in my head. *He was cheating on me with the girl at the Marilyn Manson concert and she's pregnant; he thinks I'm gross and fat after having a kid and he wants to leave me; he's fallen in love with the new girl at work because she's young and fun and skinny with Julia Roberts hair*. The possibilities in my head were endless.

I started mentally preparing for every possible scenario that could cause him to be this upset. I was almost relieved when he said, "I think I'm bisexual." Bisexual. *Is that all?* I thought, sighing in relief. I grew up around all kinds of people. It wasn't a big deal to me, but Frank grew up in a very different household, so I knew this *was* a big deal to him. I grabbed his hands and I kissed them. I pulled him into me and told him that it didn't matter to me. Then I asked him if he loved me, to which he replied, "Of course!" As if I'd just asked him if the sky was really blue. I knew he'd say that, so I smiled. Then I told him that he was amazing, and one of the best things to ever happen to me, that it didn't matter if he was bisexual, because he loved me and that choosing me over a man was no different than choosing me over a woman. He cried even harder. What I thought would've made him feel better only seemed to make him feel worse, and that's when my Spidey-sense started tingling.

Was there more?

I pulled away from our embrace, and I asked him if he was sure he was bisexual and not gay. He stopped crying and cupped my face. "I'm sure," he said. "One hundred percent. I love you, Lori. You are who I want to be with. This is just something that's always bothered me." Then he kissed me. It wasn't just a peck either, I'm talking one of the most passion-ate kisses we'd shared throughout our entire marriage, and it didn't end there. I'd gotten my answer.

Only now I was starting to wonder if I'd gotten the full answer. We got back home, and I started working on myself.

I lost weight and thought I was getting my sexy back. I tried new hairstyles, bought sexier clothes, hell, I tried no clothes. Still, he was always tired, or he wasn't feeling well. Finally, I went back to that conversation and thought that maybe I should bring it up again. Something was going on.

I don't remember exactly how I brought the conversation up, but knowing me, I probably just said, "Hey, remember how you said you thought you were bisexual? Have you ever thought about acting on that?" Looking back now, by this point, deep down I knew that Frank and I weren't going to stay together forever. So did he. Neither of us was wanted to admit it, but I needed him to say this now to make it real. To make this moment real. If he didn't, I could still cling to the delusion. I could still pretend that everything was fine. I knew things weren't fine. I knew that he wasn't bisexual, and I knew that our lives would never be the same. But he didn't say it. And I didn't want to let go, not yet, so I suggested an open marriage—anything to avoid what we both knew was inevitable.

I have no real explanation for why I did this. Well, no *rational* explanation, anyway. Maybe I was trying to gauge the temperature of our relationship? We weren't having sex, and we were barely kissing. Something was off for us sexually, but in every other way, Frank was the perfect partner. On top of being a solid provider, he was a fantastic dad and my biggest supporter. I had started writing again now that Aaliyah was about a year old and was toying with the idea of going back to school to perfect my craft. I had always regretted how I just left and never finished. Something that was once so important to me, thrown away on a whim. Frank supported my decision, so I went back. We were closer than ever in every way but one. I suppose part of my way of supplementing that loss was to open the marriage—or maybe it was my way of refusing to let go.

When we first spoke about an open marriage, his biggest fear was that the first time he slept with a man, he'd find out that he preferred it. He told me this during the discussion, not after. I knew full well going into this arrangement that he was afraid he might enjoy being with a man more than a woman, and I still went along with it. Why be with someone who doesn't want to be with you? That was my thought process going in; that was how I reckoned with making the decision. Of course, at the time I naïvely thought our love was so strong that no matter who either of us slept with, we'd come back to one another. I opened the marriage for him, but to be fair I thought I should get out there too, just in case.

So we downloaded all the dating apps and made each other profiles. It was exciting! I hadn't gone on a date in ten years. Even when Frank and I were dating, they weren't "grown up" dates. No fancy dinners sipping wine and playing footsie under the tables like you see the adults do on TV. Nope, we were slouching in Denny's booths unzipping our jeans because we ate too much. Occasionally we went to the Cheesecake Factory, but that was a rare treat! No, this was my Carrie Bradshaw moment. I was in my thirties now, so I had to date like a grown-up...using Tinder...ha!

I never actually made it on a date. I'd get a match, talk to the guy, get creeped out by his eagerness, and then delete the app. I was married already and wasn't really interesting in going through all that. It was a fun idea to me, but that's all it was. An idea. To Frank, it was very different. He carefully selected photos, put thought into his bio, and carried on conversations for more than a day. He was very serious, but this was for him after all, so I expected that. I went on about my days as usual, getting the kids up and ready for school, seeing him off to work, making my pot of coffee, and sitting down to begin my own schoolwork from home. Nothing had really changed for me after that conversation, but everything had changed for him.

One day he came home as I was cooking what my kids consider my specialty: macaroni and cheese, mashed potatoes, broccoli, and baked pork chops. I won't lie and say I'm an amazing chef or anything, but my food is flavorful and edible. He seemed excited about something, so I waited for him to tell me. We had dinner, and nothing. Watched a movie, nothing. We watched *Master Chef*, nothing! During *The Great British Baking Show*, I finally exploded. "What are you so happy about today?" He smiled looking up from his phone and just froze for a moment.

"What?" I pushed.

"I think I'm gonna do it. I'm gonna go meet a guy tonight."

Now, most women would start to nope out of this whole open marriage right there (or not enter it in the first place), but I'm not most women. I got excited!

I demanded he show me the guy. (He wasn't what I expected, but this wasn't about me.) Then I asked about his job, where he was from, was he openly out. He gave me the rundown, and then we started to get him ready. I can't remember whether or not the guy was out himself, but I do remember that he'd told Frank he had never done anything with a man before. He told Frank that they would just make out and get to know each other.

"It's not a big deal," he said, as I sat on the edge of the bathtub watching my husband get ready to go out with another man, but it *was* a big deal. I wish I had an explanation for why I was so cool about it all, why it took so long for me to process what was really happening. Maybe I was in shock? I was definitely in denial. Even when we prepare for the worst, it doesn't mean that we're ready to handle it, that we even *can* handle it.

Whatever it was, it was in full force, as I sat there in this moment with genuine excitement for him. I'd had gay and lesbian friends since high school, and I understood how hard coming to terms with your sexuality could be, so my natural response was to support him. I've always been the kind of person who wants to make everybody happy. The people pleaser. I want everyone to live their full potential, to exist as the best version of themselves possible. I just wanted to love on and take care of everyone. The only problem with that was that I often forgot to love and take care of myself. I forgot to put myself first every once in a while. I had gotten so used to supporting and helping everyone else that I no longer remembered how to do so for myself. Maybe it was easier that way. You know how people can always see the issues in someone else's situation but are oblivious to their own? I think it kind of works the same way.

It's so much easier to be there for other people. If you're constantly holding up everyone else in your life, you don't have time to notice that you're falling. That's me. It's easier to help a friend working through a difficult time in life than it is to acknowledge my own struggles—to face my own reality. I don't even like to talk about my difficulties out loud. My life can be an actual shit show, but when my mom calls to check on me, "I'm doing fabulous, Mom, how are *you*?!" It just seems so much easier to deal alone, but it only *seems* that way. What I've come to learn is that when you keep everything inside, it builds up, and I had a lot of buildup.

So there I was, lying in my empty king-sized bed listening to *The Office* and watching the clock. He'd left the house around 9:30, and 10:30 had come quickly. So had 11:30, and then midnight. I told myself that Frank was having fun, so it didn't matter how late he was out. This was something he needed to do. I thought about some of my friends who had been unable to come out to their own families, and sometimes to themselves. I was happy to give him this opportunity to explore his sexual identity. It didn't even occur to me what this would really mean for our marriage. I rolled over and finally resigned myself to getting some sleep when I heard the front door open. I wanted to sit up, but I didn't want to seem eager, so I just lay there.

I heard Frank set the keys on the table downstairs, and then walk to the fridge. The fridge door closed, and I could hear him making his way upstairs, so I closed my eyes. When he reached the top of the stairs, he entered our bedroom doorway, and his feet stopped. I fluttered my eyes open and did my best fake yawn.

"You're back already?" I was putting on my best performance.

"Yeah," he responded dryly and began to undress.

I sat up. "How was it?"

"It was okay."

He pulled off his shoes, then his socks. I rolled closer to the edge of the bed.

"Just okay? What all did you do?"

He took his shirt off. "I mean, we did everything."

Everything?!

"Everything? What's everything?"

He seemed indifferent. "I mean everything. Kissed... had sex."

I shot up. "You had sex?!"

His cool-guy demeanor broke and he laughed.

"Yes, we had sex."

Apparently, it had quickly become obvious that it wasn't his date's first rodeo. He was a pro. One thing led to another and *boom*. Sex. I'll spare you the intimate details, but I asked and he answered. At the end of the conversation, and after he showered, we lay in our bed together. He seemed content, for the first time in a long time. He pulled me into him and wrapped both arms around me. Frank wasn't a cuddler. Never had been, but that night, he cuddled me so tight that I had to adjust several times to breathe. Before he went to sleep, he kissed the top of my head and asked me to look him in the eye.

"Thank you for this. I really do appreciate it."

I smiled and said goodnight. I don't know if it was realization creeping in or what, but for the first time since all of this began, I started to feel uneasy. It was nothing like what would come later, but it was enough to give me trouble getting to sleep that night. I was still thinking about it the next morning in the kitchen as I made my cup of coffee.

Later that night—it might have been a few nights later, time starts to merge for me here—I needed to know. Even though I was back at school now, my marriage was all I could think of. I saw the end approaching rapidly, and instead of slowing down and approaching with caution, I put my foot on the gas and went full force.

"Are you gay?"

It came out one night as we were making dinner. I waited for him to say it out loud. He stared at me, and I stared back at him. We stayed frozen like that for what felt like an eternity. Then finally he said the words.

"Yes, I'm gay."

My whole world should have come crashing down. I should've called it quits then and there. I'd read stories about what other women did when their husbands or long-term boyfriends came out. There was a whole range of emotional response that would've been expected and understandable. Instead, I smiled. No, it was worse than that. I gasped, smiled, and threw my arms around my husband, screaming congratulations as if he'd just told me he'd gotten a promotion at work. I'm cringing now as I think about how blissfully naïve I was. I cannot even begin to describe the motivation behind my reaction. Maybe it was a defense mechanism? More shock? More denial? Love? I just remember being so excited for him to finally say it out loud for the first time in his entire life, and as we hugged, he cried. I could tell this was extremely hard for him. He didn't want to be gay, but he couldn't help it; he was born that way.

A lifetime of homophobic teachings had taught him that it was wrong, that *he* was wrong. Imagine growing up and being judged for the way you stand or place your hands. By your parents, the first people we learn to love. Having them question you about whether you like boys or girls as early as five or six. That's why I was happy for him. My parents were not like that. My extended family was not like that. When it came to a person's sexuality, our family motto was, "If you like it, I love it."

Frank wasn't afforded the freedom to find himself. I loved him. He was my best friend, so it was very easy for me to sympathize with him and support him fully on his journey. In some ways I could perhaps even relate. I didn't have the freedom to experience things that most people experience in high school. I understood what it was like not to have something that it seems everyone else does. The only problem was, I didn't acknowledge the journey that I would be facing. The way he grew up and the struggles he faced were awful, but it did not negate what I was going through and the struggle that I was now about to face. But at the time, I thought it did. I thought his struggle was bigger, more important. Or maybe I was just choosing to focus on fixing his drama and refusing to face my own. I was a professional at helping others—not so much myself.

Soon enough, the celebration was over. We were over. For some reason, I couldn't cry—not at first. I shed tears in tiny spurts, during showers and bathroom trips, but I couldn't cry like I'd wanted to with big ugly tears and loud painful sobs. The huge, pressure-relieving waterworks I longed for just wouldn't come. He was gay. Even after he'd said it, I didn't believe it. Not really. I didn't want to. I'm honestly not sure what I thought—that maybe he really was bi and would realize that. That maybe he would see just how irreplaceable my love was and not be able to walk away. But would I want that? Should I want that? A gay man to stay with me, with no real sexual attraction to me whatsoever. Could I happily exist in a relationship where I could never be wanted the way a straight man wants a woman? Never be desired by the man I've devoted my life to? Never feeling sexually desired, by someone I still loved? Did I really want that? Did I deserve more than that?

I wasn't so sure anymore. I wasn't sure about anything. Throughout our relationship, Frank had been an attentive husband. Of course, in retrospect we could've had sex more (or even kissed more). I remember in those early years of marriage, long after the novelty of new sex had worn off, he was always so worried about losing his hair, and frequently stated that it was a sign of low testosterone. Perhaps that explained his low sex drive? We were able to rationalize everything, because I had nothing to compare it to.

What I thought was a romantic fairytale ended up being my kryptonite. If I had dated other people, perhaps I would've noticed how unconventional our romantic relationship really was. Instead, I thought that maybe it was me, maybe something was wrong with *me*. I would do my best to entice him, but he was always too tired. I just knew it *had* to be me. I was no longer attractive to him. Always worried about my looks, I started to see things wrong with me too.

But none of it mattered. Frank was gay. I could've gone under the knife and emerged an exact replica of Beyoncé, and it wouldn't have made any difference. I remember feeling so stupid in those early days, still wanting him to desire me. To want to be married to me. To want our family. One day, that pathetic hope morphed into anger. Almost overnight. I just woke up one morning and decided that I hated him. I didn't hate him because he was gay, but I hated him because he lied about it. Who does that? Who gets married to someone, knowing they are questioning their sexuality? Who stays with that person for ten years, and has three children with them? I felt disgusted. And pissed.

I decided to write him a letter, telling him about how he stole the best years of my life and ruined me for anyone else.

Who wants a thirty-two-year-old single woman with three very young children? I was damaged goods, and he was the buyer who damaged me, only to throw me into a Goodwill donation box to be messed over by any fool who likes to tinker with broken things. I cried as I typed up the letter. I was telling him exactly how I felt, and if I knew Frank, when he read this letter, he'd feel sorry. He'd feel sorry, and he'd come back, and we'd go to therapy and figure this out. In all my plotting, I never stopped to ask myself why I wanted him back, why I needed him back. Was it the comfort? The inability to face family and friends who believed we were this great couple? The fear of being alone? All of the above? I don't know what it was, but I do know it kept me from telling anyone in my life what was going on. I needed to work through this myself.

I sent the letter via text and watched for the word "delivered" to change to "read." It did. Now, I waited. Waited in my room for any movement to come from his—any signal of receipt. After a few minutes, the three dots appeared. He was responding. I sat there, feeling content with the letter I'd written. Content with my level of vulnerability. Sure of the fact that this would bring him back to me. We could go to therapy. We could work this out. If any couple could survive this, it was us. Imagine my surprise when those three dots revealed what Frank had been writing. He was not apologetic, but conciliatory. He accused me of sending him mixed messages, of pretending to be okay with everything when I wasn't, and that it wasn't fair.

Fair? How dare *he* tell *me* what wasn't fair?

I felt sorry for myself a lot during those days. I was abandoned. I'd mope around the house, using his guilt to my advantage. It wasn't fair that he did this to me, so he had to pay. All the things he'd normally refuse to do became his penance. He hated going out to dinner with the kids. We have great kids (I promise I'm not just saying that), but for some reason, eating in public where other people could see them flipped a switch. They would argue and scream, and I completely understood why he didn't want to go out with them. However, he had broken me, so he had to take us out now. And he had to sit next to the kids, while I enjoyed my dinner for a change. If I wanted a two-hour bath, he would have to stop whatever he was doing and keep an eye on them while I disappeared for some me time. If we wanted to watch a movie together, it had to be one I chose. It was all about me, until it wasn't. Until that text.

I read what he said at least three times. *I* wasn't being fair to *him*? Was what he did fair to me? I wasted the best years of my life trying to work on a marriage that was doomed from the start, and he *knew*. It wasn't like he woke up one day and realized he was gay. He told me that he'd felt this way for as long as he could remember. So, he walked down the aisle with me, knowing he was attracted to men sexually. He dated me, knowing he was attracted to men sexually. He met my family, introduced me to his, all while knowing he was attracted to men sexually. I honestly didn't want to hear this bullshit about being fair, because what about any of this had been fair to me?

That's pretty much what I wrote back. You know his response? He apologized. He agreed that it wasn't fair. That he hadn't been fair. I wanted a fight. I didn't want him to agree with me. I wanted him to come at me with the same anger that I'd thrown at him, so that I could really let him have it. We had been together for ten years, and I knew every button to push to hurt him. I needed his anger to signal that part in my brain that controlled my tact, and let it know that it was time to disable it. But he didn't bite. He just apologized, over and over and over again. What a waste of perfectly good anger.

As I reread his apology, I went back to Frank's original response. *Was I being unfair?* I thought back to how excited I was for him when he came out to me. How excited I was helping him go on his first date. How I had encouraged him to come out, to tell me about everything, to share this experience with me every step of the way. I wanted to be in his corner, but at some point, I realized I couldn't be. Not all the way. I needed to be in my corner. I needed to snap out of this deep denial and deal with the truth. Frank wasn't bisexual. He was gay. He loved me in the best way that he could, but it would never be the way I wanted to be loved. The way I loved *him*. This was not going to work. No amount of therapy could fix this.

You'd think that would have been my wake-up call, but it wasn't. After that, I operated under the irrational belief that I was somehow special. That even if Frank did identify as gay, I'd be the one woman he could want. Sexuality is fluid, so even if he liked men 99 percent of the time, I was the percent that mattered. I convinced myself that I was the mystical woman, and I started asking him every day, obsessively, if he was sure he was all the way gay.

"Give me a percentage," I'd ask casually, while I was loading the dishwasher and he was mixing his pre-workout. At first, he played along.

"I'd say between seventy-five and eighty percent."

Good. I have a chance. I could still turn things around.

"Cool," was my casual response, but internally I was nurturing a tiny flame of hope. I started trying to be more romantic.

I'd make sure the house was spotless and his favorite dinners were on the table. The idea was that he'd eventually realize he wasn't going to find anyone like me, in male or female form. I was one of a kind.

About a month later, I had genuinely convinced myself that things were headed back to normal. After our (one-sided) text argument, we decided to stay married and just see where things went. He hadn't gone out on any more dates after his first burst of freedom. He was barely even on the apps anymore. Had he gotten it out of his system? I thought that maybe we'd be fine, that our family would be fine. I wasn't prepared for what was coming. One day, he told me he'd been talking to a guy and was gonna go out. Nothing serious, just a "casual encounter."

"Okay, yeah, cool."

"I'm not going out until after the kids are asleep. Around eleven or twelve."

I nodded. "Sounds good."

We didn't talk about it much more after that. I don't think I saw a picture of him then, but I would later. Frank went out after the kids had been long knocked out, and I sat in the living room watching TV. I told him goodbye, and I didn't think about it anymore. I had convinced myself that things were okay, despite them being very far from it. Frank wasn't gone long, maybe an hour. When he came back, he sat down next to me on the couch and was visibly excited.

"How was it?"

Why did I ask?

"He was amazing!" Frank beamed. "We're gonna see each other again sometime this week."

Wait, I thought this was a casual, one-off hookup?

179

"Oh wow! How exciting? Tell me about him."

And he did. If I hadn't been in such denial, maybe I would've seen this for what it was. He was falling in love. His first same-sex love.

He was falling hard, and I couldn't see it. Even he couldn't see it. We were both living in this delusion that we could somehow have an open marriage. Sometime after his first few encounters with this new guy, a while after my angry text, we had a long talk and decided that if we wanted this to work, an open marriage would be the only way. He would do his thing, I would do my thing, and it wouldn't interfere with what we had. If I had been paying attention, I would've seen where this was going. It was the beginning of the end. Not the end of my marriage, that was already over despite my attempts at life-saving efforts. This was the beginning of the end of my delusions. I was finally about to move on from shock and denial. As we all know, grief isn't linear, so three guesses where I go next?

13

Survivor

I became a bitch. I'm not proud of my behavior, but it's the truth. I was the queen of mixed signals; I would act like everything was okay when Frank wasn't going out, then when he was, I'd get angry. It was an anger I didn't even know I had in me. I'd send him texts telling him how he ruined my life. I knew it was his greatest wound, and I'd poke it every time I felt that anger bubbling up inside me. He still loved me deeply, and whenever he thought I was moving on, I'd remind him of just how much I wasn't. I'd remind him of how I almost died birthing his child. I'd tell him that it *was* his fault that I'd gone crazy after all.

I'd tell him that he wasn't a good father. That he was too busy going out and enjoying his new gay lifestyle to be a good father. I told him that his children would hate him for ruining our marriage—that everyone would hate him for doing this to me. Then, in between my outbursts, I'd apologize. I'd say

I was going through something, so just let me go through it. Both sides were sincere, but that didn't make it any better.

I was embarrassed. This marriage, our family, was the *one* thing that I had *felt* I'd done right. I wasn't ready to let go of the illusion. I started to feel like my life had gotten away from me, pinpointing the start to right after the move to California. Almost everything that I had tried had failed—until I became a wife and mother. That was something I had started and completed. It was *my* success that I had worked hard for, and now he had taken that away from me.

We moved to a new house that offered more division. It was split so that we wouldn't have to see each other if we didn't want to, but we would still essentially be living together for the kids. It was there that I decided two things: 1) I wanted a divorce; and 2) I wanted to get back out there. While number two was an epic fail—too much, too soon—number one was attainable, and we started there. I started the paperwork despite Frank not wanting the divorce. He begged to keep the open-marriage dream alive, but it had been dead on arrival. He didn't resist, set on giving me what I had decided I wanted. Part of me still wonders if it was his way of staying in the closet, but I never asked him. I hadn't told anyone. He asked me not to, so I didn't. It helped that I wasn't exactly ready to have that conversation. Then...something changed.

I was depressed, though not like the other times. I didn't want to disappear, but I did want to move past this already. I wanted to go around the pain, when what I actually needed was to go through it. I was taking this class, Critical Thinking and Argument, and one session our professor, Dr. Shane Underwood, came onto the Zoom and shared with us that he was going through a breakup. I remember hearing the way he spoke about the process, and thinking to myself how beautiful it was that he had the strength to get the fuck up and go *through* it. It sucked, yeah, and he let himself sit with that, but he kept going. That moment was powerful for me. For the first time, I shared that I, too, was going through a breakup...a divorce. He expressed his empathy, and we moved on with the class.

I felt empowered after that moment of validation. I was ready to start the work of going *through* the process. It wasn't great, even though I knew the divorce was the right thing to do. The tears finally came. I finally let them. I finally let myself accept that the marriage was truly over. In April of 2021, Frank and I signed the divorce agreement, and about three months later, the divorce was final. We went to court on Zoom and told the judge that we were irrevocably broken. And then it was official. I was divorced.

It would still be a while before we told anyone. But life was better. I stopped trying to rekindle the flame of a candle that had no wick. I put my energy into my kids, into school, and into myself. Frank and I still lived together, but like roommates. I would take long spa days once a month and just let everything go. I even went on a few dates. I was slowly but surely finding myself, something I had never stopped to do. I had gone from living with my family to living with Frank— during a time where I was still trying to find my place in life. I had been happy as a wife and mother, but I also sensed something was missing: *me*. The true me, the me who knew who she was and what she wanted in life. The me who existed outside of my family of origin, outside of Frank and his family, outside of our kids. I was figuring that all out now, and it felt good.

A few months later, we told the children that Mommy and Daddy were divorced. They took it as well as could be expected. AJ cried, and then Ali and Aaliyah cried because he was crying. AJ was seven, the only one who truly understood at the time. I don't remember what was said, because I let Frank do the talking. I just cried off to the side the entire time.

After telling the kids, we told our families. I told Keke first, and she was extremely supportive. She had words of encouragement for both me and Frank. My parents took it okay (I'm 99.999 percent sure Keke had already told them) and offered me words of encouragement. Lawrencia was ready to fight Frank. When she saw that I wasn't, she loosened up and told me to have a hot girl summer. My brother took it the worst. Lawrence had a lot of questions that made me uncomfortable to answer. He was the last one I told, and the conversation left me feeling everything all over again.

I remember I had a class after the conversation. I don't know why I arranged it that way. I hadn't finished the homework, and after the call I was a wreck. I figured I'd still go, because it was another class with Dr. Underwood, and his lectures were always a good time—just what I needed. I decided I would just take the L and move on. Well, he started the class by calling out everyone who hadn't done the homework for wasting his time, as well as our own. I was already vulnerable, so I immediately logged off. In tears, I emailed him apologizing for wasting everyone's time. Everything that had happened earlier in the day spilled out into the email. I told him that I'd get my shit together and come correct next week. He responded during the class break, saying that I should come back on the Zoom. That someone might say something I needed to hear, or that I might say something someone else needed to hear. Then he offered to listen during his office hours, and he did.

I told him *everything* I had been going through, and he listened without judgment. I rambled on, thankful that none of my classmates had decided to attend office hours that day. He listened as I talked and talked, hoping I was making sense. He interjected occasionally, but mostly he just listened. It was like therapy. When I finally finished, he shared words of encouragement, and offered me a second chance at the assignment. I went home, and I think I finished it that night.

School went on, life went on, and I had this strange feeling of serenity. I wasn't hiding anything, so I became less withdrawn with people. I was talking to my family more, reaching out to friends I had stopped talking to during the divorce and the events leading up to it. Frank and his new partner were getting serious, and the fact that he was moving on so soon pissed me off. I was being bitchy again, and I knew what that meant.

It was time to make my exit.

I moved back home to be with my family. Frank didn't want us to leave. We alternated crying as I packed up my life and prepared to start over. The kids were excited to live with Grandma and Pawpaw. It didn't hit them that Dad wasn't staying until he left for his flight back to Atlanta after spending two days helping us get settled in. AJ was no longer mad at him, and they had all gotten used to the idea of us being divorced. Frank never gave up on trying to resume their close relationship. The more AJ resisted, the more love he gave. Eventually, when AJ was ready, they were back together like they never left. AJ even told me I needed to get back out there. One night, I was getting ready to go out with friends and had done my makeup. It had been a while since I felt like doing it. I dressed my best, wearing a skintight black dress that accentuated the shape of my legs. I remember looking at myself in the mirror and thinking, *You're not so bad.*

"Are you going out, Mom?" AJ asked.

I zoomed into the mirror trying to apply my eyeliner correctly. My eyesight is horrendous, even up close, without my glasses, so I always hated this part.

"Yes, but only for a little while."

My daughters hated me leaving the house. They couldn't comprehend why I'd ever want to leave the house, let alone without them. But AJ was usually more independent.

He shuffled his feet, "Are you going on a date?"

"What?! No!" I suppose my appearance did give "date" more than "girls' night."

"Why not?"

"Because."

"Because why?"

I closed the cap to the eyeliner and put my glasses back on to observe the damage.

"Do you want me to go on a date, Son?"

It always makes people laugh that I call him Son, but he *is* my son. He calls me Mom, I call him Son. Unless he's acting up, then he's Alex Jake.

He thought about the question, "Yes."

"Why?"

He smiled, "Because you're really pretty, and I think you should have a boyfriend."

I gave him a hug and told him I loved him. Mommy wasn't ready for a boyfriend, but it didn't matter, because the handsomest man in the world had called her pretty. It was Mariska Hargitay all over again.

The kids were in school now, except for Aaliyah. I would be home in my office (the kitchen table) doing Zoom classes, and she would be at the table with me, eating her snacks and watching *Gabby's Dollhouse*. Then we'd walk and pick up the kids, do their homework, and then I'd work on *mine* while they played in the room my parents had designated the "play area." Living with my parents was amazing. I didn't think I'd enjoy it so much.

My dad had literally built a playground in the backyard for the kids, and they would play out there for hours. There was a huge window in the kitchen facing the backyard, so I didn't even have to sit in the heat to watch them. My dad has an active social life, so he was always out. Sometimes he'd cook before he left, but when he didn't my mom and I had fun. We'd order DoorDash and watch movies with the kids until they (and my mom) passed out.

I was a few months into the move when I left to go film *Claim to Fame*, a reality show I had "auditioned" for a while back. Someone sent me a message on Instagram, that looked like 100 percent spam, about a new reality show on celebrity relatives. I noticed we had mutual friends, and after verifying they were an actual human who worked in casting, I went along with it. I was fresh off a divorce and in my "try something new" era. Why not? With the COVID Delta strain roaming around, production kept getting pushed back, until I had forgotten all about it. But it hadn't forgotten about me. When I got the call to come film, I wanted to back out, but my entire family, including Frank, refused to let me. My parents would keep the kids so they could stay in school, and Frank would fly in every other weekend. They worked it all out without me. I guess they were *all* tired of me choosing to be invisible.

The producers put us up in a hotel, took our phones, laptops, IDs, everything. The only things we could keep were the books we had brought with us to read. I had brought Clive Barker's *Books of Blood*, all volumes. At around nine o'clock that first night, after they'd brought our dinner to us, my stomach started to ache. I thought it was nerves, so I tried to calm myself. By midnight, the pain had become so unbearable that I couldn't be still. It was like I *needed* to move. As a recovering hypochondriac, I decided that I could be dying, so I needed to call someone. Then it hit me—they took my fucking *phone*.

They'd mentioned we couldn't call anyone from the hotel phone because it had been disconnected, but something told me to check. I was strictly informed that I could not leave the room under any circumstances, but if the phone didn't work, I'd have to. I wasn't going to die in this damn hotel room.

I picked up the phone, and there was a dial tone. I pushed the button labeled front desk.

"Hello, front desk."

I had no idea who to ask for.

"Hi, uh, I'm with the reality show. I'm having a medical emergency, and I don't know who to call."

"One moment."

Apparently, he knew who to call, because moments later, when I was at the point of tears, someone knocked on my door to take me to the ER. I threw up twice on the walk to the car, and prayed I wouldn't do it *in* the car. I didn't. We made it to the ER, and it took forever to be seen by a doctor. I was writhing around in excruciating pain, but they couldn't give me anything until after I had an MRI. That took forever as well.

Finally, I had the MRI, which revealed gallstones. I was having a gallbladder attack. They gave me morphine, and I was able to sleep until it wore off. They sent me home with strong painkillers that I could take if it happened again before I could get my gallbladder removed. It was after my hair and makeup call time by the time I had been released, so I literally ran to my room, showered quickly, and ran right into hair and makeup.

For those of you who haven't seen the show, *Claim to Fame* is a house reality competition show. All of the contestants were related to celebrities, but we didn't know who. The point was to figure out everyone else before they figured *you* out. I didn't expect to win, or even make the finale. I just didn't want to be the first one out. My siblings had all warned me of the secondhand embarrassment it would inflict on them. Keke thought I would win. I thought she was being kind.

That first night, I was a ball of nerves. The day had been fun, getting my hair and makeup done, doing interviews, and just soaking it all in, but after they let us into the house, the game had begun. I looked around the room—this was my competition. I had hoped to make friends, but I wondered, did they feel the same? What if this turned cutthroat? What had I gotten myself into?

I was immediately drawn to Pepper, who always came off as authentically Pepper. She was witty, hilarious, and genuinely kind. For a while I thought she was related to John Candy, but later found out she was Dean Martin's granddaughter. It was obvious to me that Louise was related to Simone Biles. I loved her personality. She reminded me of Lawrencia. Amara (Whoopie Goldberg's granddaughter) was always cranked up to eleven. Brittany (Brett Favre's daughter) seemed kind, but strategic (while she *was* strategic, I can confirm that she is also extremely kind and was a lifesaver when I began my first semester as a Teacher's Assistant). I didn't spend much time with Michael (Zendaya's cousin), but he was in game mode to a fault, so I avoided him. Dominique (Al Sharpton's daughter) and Kai (Tiffany Haddish's sister) intimidated me. They had both come to play, and it showed. X (Laverne Cox's twin brother) was a beautiful soul. I hated that I didn't get to spend more time with him. Max (Chuck Norris's grandson) was such a joy to be around. He was the first to get eliminated, and I wished we could've had him around longer. Logan (who was the cousin of country music singer Jason Aldean) became my partner in crime, but we didn't talk much initially. I had overheard him and Louise on night one talking about the film *Joyful Noise* and how they loved Keke Palmer. I knew I had to avoid them. I ended up rooming with my house bestie Lark (Cindy Crawford's niece) and Dominique, which was fine with me, considering it had a master bathroom that was fit for three queens.

It's funny, after the show, everyone came up to me telling me that they loved my strategy, but I didn't really have one. Well, not until the final six. Up until that point, I was enjoying the moment—*my* moment. I had just gone through a divorce and was trying something new. I wanted to reinvent myself, do all the things I had previously been too insecure to do. I never saw myself singing in front of an audience on national television, or jumping in a pool to find lettered balls, or walking the runaway in a fashion show.

That fashion show was a full circle moment. I have never been a fashionista. I can't tell the difference between high fashion and Target. I was having a full-blown panic attack.

One of the producers backstage, Mackie, had to reel me in. She said, "You're the closer! Close this show!" As cliché as it sounds, I heard her. She was right, this *was* my show, the show of my life, and I had to decide how to close that chapter of being the quiet girl afraid to trust her own thoughts and opinions, afraid to get out there and try new things, make new experiences. The girl who was so proud of everyone around her, but too afraid to be proud of herself, too afraid to do something that she *would* be proud of. Too afraid to risk failing, too committed to playing it safe, taking the easy road. In that moment, I remembered every lesson Tyra Banks ever gave on *ANTM*. That girl needed to be closed, and so I walked out onto that runway, and I closed the show.

I was never the star in my own life. I wasn't even a main character. I was that character actor everyone knows by face alone. I was a support system for everyone. And I was happy with that role, until I wasn't. During filming, after I was in the final six, it was like a switch flipped. Up until that point, I wasn't *really* playing. I was just excited for the experience, and meeting the people. I didn't care about winning. I cared about saying I did something that was completely outside of my comfort zone. But now, I wanted to *win*. Why *couldn't* I win? Once I started to see myself winning, I started to see myself doing a lot of things. I started seeing them not just as dreams, but as possibilities. I didn't have to close the show on just being happy to be there. I could go for more. I deserved to give myself the opportunity to go for more.

On the day of the finale, I told myself: *Win or lose, your life changes after this.*

As it turned out...I won. I literally closed the show.

Epilogue

I was hesitant to write this book. I wasn't sure if I was at a point where what I had to say about what I've been through would even mean anything to anyone other than me. I didn't know if I had learned any valuable lesson, if I had come to some grand conclusion. It was when I accepted that I hadn't figured everything out that I decided to share my story. It's impossible to have everything figured out—we just don't live long enough.

I spent years feeling bitter about moving to California, blaming my parents for a stolen high school experience, but did that even matter in the grand scheme of things? I was so focused on what I was missing, that I didn't stop to think about what I was gaining. California had so much to offer, but only when I was ready to accept it.

California is my home now, but so is Chicago—the *me* that sits before you today couldn't exist if it weren't for the time spent in both places. I have fond and painful memories of both. It was all necessary to make me who I am today.

So, who am I today?

To some people, I'm Loreal. To others, I'm LC. To the ones who really know me, I'm Lori or Luri. To my parents, I'm Lori

Tori. I'm all of those wrapped into one. I took a theory class, and we studied Freud's concept of the fragmented self, and I've never had a stronger sense of my identity. I don't agree with it all, but that part stuck with me. Each one of those pieces, each part that I choose to display, all belong to me. It's not being fake or phony, it's choosing which side of yourself to display today at this particular moment. I can be Loreal the daughter, I can be Loreal the mommy, Loreal the big sister, Loreal the student, and during summers and winters, I can transform into Florida LoLo and do hoodrat things with my friends.

Following the divorce and *Claim to Fame*, I took a long hard look at my life. I asked myself, if you had to do one job, outside of motherhood, for the rest of your life, what would it be? I deliberated over this for some time. I was given a second chance, like a reboot of your favorite sitcom, and I wasn't about to waste it. I wanted to write, but I wanted something outside of that as well.

I thought about that first semester at Pasadena City College. How I'd felt like I belonged. I wanted to do something with education. I thought again about maybe teaching ninth-grade English, because I loved my ninth-grade English teacher. Then I remembered that I didn't really want to teach teenagers. Love them, but I don't want to be their authority figure. I was taking a lot of English classes at the time, learning about a lot of philosophers that I'd heard of but never really explored.

Initially, I went back to school to learn the craft of creative writing, but I found myself drawn to theory. Ever since that 1C class, where we covered hermeneutics, I found myself hungry to know more. I kept taking those classes, even though I didn't need them. I found myself in Introduction to Literary Theory and Criticism, and that's when I knew what I wanted to do with my life with the utmost certainty. I had toyed with the idea before, but this cemented it. The struggling to understand Lacan and his three registers had assured me of my path: I wanted to be an English professor. I wanted to learn, and then pass that knowledge on to others. Maybe inspire someone the way my professor had inspired me.

So that's what I'm working towards these days. I have this fancy dream of being an English professor during the school year, and during the summers I can work on a short story anthology, because that's what I want to write: short horror stories. Yeah, it's a dream, but it's *my* dream—one I carved out for myself. Sometimes I wish I had arrived at this point sooner, especially when I attempt to juggle being a mom and a student, but then I remember that the only reason I *can* do so well now is because I went through some shit. Every minute of my life has led to this moment, and if it had come any sooner, it might not have gone as well. I'm genuinely happy as I struggle through some of these classes. I wouldn't change anything in the world.

I wouldn't change Frank being gay. I think what happened needed to happen. In retrospect I shouldn't have gotten married so soon and rushed into creating a family. I wasn't ready. While there were easier ways to learn this lesson, I'm glad it went this way. Our kids are amazing. They are intuitive, empathetic, and inclusive, qualities that are more necessary these days than ever.

In my late twenties, I often found myself looking back to the "good old days." I'd remember living with my family in that mansion during my first semesters of college. The parties we threw, the times we spent traveling. I used to miss those days like crazy. These days, I think about the old days, but it's not a longing. I'm not *missing* anything. Frank and I are great co-parents, and believe it or not, we are the best of friends. We're closer now than ever before. My relationship with my siblings is ridiculously strong. We're planning our next turn up as I write this book.

My parents are my idols, and my biggest inspiration. They drove four children across the country on a wing and a prayer. People thought they were crazy, but they did it anyway. That's how I want to live my life, doing the things that *I* want to do no matter how scary it may seem, because that's the *point* of life. My mom would sometimes say to me when I was in my early twenties and feeling lost, "My life didn't really start until I was in my thirties. That was when I really started to have the confidence to do a lot of the stuff I had only ever dreamt about because I was just always so worried about what that big leap would look like." Now, in my thirties, I get it. In my thirties, I've noticed that I don't really have much time these days for the "what ifs." Things either will work out, or they won't, and when they don't there's always some way to maneuver and readjust. And if there isn't you may need to maneuver the entire plan, which is also fine. Starting over isn't this awful thing that we all like to think it is. Starting over is just another opportunity to accomplish your goals. It can be scary, sure, but so can staying on a path that's going nowhere. Or worse, leading you to a brick wall.

My professor once shared with us a quote (I can't remember from who, and I'm far too comfortable in my bed to go look now) that I'd like to paraphrase (hopefully with accuracy) for you: "Nobody can die your death." If I'm understanding this correctly, what that means is that when my time comes, I'm the only person who is able to answer that call. So naturally, I should be the only one who gets to *live* my life as well. It took me a long time to understand that. We only get this one life, and that means that we have to live it in a way that fills us with the most passion, the most joy; just fill it with the things that actually matter. But know, that may not always be possible, and that's okay. Remember: tragic serenity. As long as we're breathing, we have an opportunity to live a really good life... and a really bad life. But then it can get super cool, then slightly shitty, followed by some mild improvement. No matter how bad it gets, it can't stay that way. Not unless you're just lying there. Yeah, I've been through some shit, but that shouldn't stop me.

I didn't die, so I just keep on living. Every day we all get to make the choice to keep living, a choice that can sometimes feel impossible to make.

You didn't die, so you just *keep living*...

Acknowledgments

So many people went into making this book possible; I simply wouldn't be here without every single one of you.

To my amazing team at Dupree Miller, Lacy Lynch, Dabney Rice, and Haley Reynolds. Thank you for believing that I had something to say even when I didn't. It's so hard to look at your life and see that it hasn't been just a series of mundane events; thank you for seeing what I couldn't. To my Post Hill Press team, Anthony Ziccardi and Adriana Senior, thank you for believing in my ability to tell my story. I have never written a book (although I've started a few), and your trust and faith in me being able to put all of this into words has been absolutely indescribable—honestly a lifelong dream. To Wenonah Hoye, I have enjoyed every single moment of working with you. You listened to me, laughed with me, and have been the voice I needed throughout all of this! Mom and Dad, thank you for every sacrifice you made on all of our behalf. Without witnessing you do the unthinkable, we wouldn't have known what greatness we could achieve. Keke, thank you for always being you no matter what. You like to call me your hero, but you are *my* hero. The way you keep going even when you feel like you can't is truly awe inspiring. You are my sister, and I *love* my sister! Lawrencia, thank you for reminding me that I can still be young and turnt! Your advice is always welcome (even when it seems a bit out there). I love watching you blossom into a beautiful young woman who doesn't comprehend the word no. Lawrence, thank you for reminding me of why I always wanted a brother. Your humor and calming nature always come when needed. You've been my running buddy since your day one on Earth—we have plenty more adventures to go, me boy! Frank, there would be no book without you. There would be no story, no realization, no understanding myself as an independent individual with her own thoughts and goals. For that I cannot thank you enough! Dr. Shane Underwood, thank you for always listening to me ramble (and sometimes cry) about this book and my life, for introducing me to the life-changing world of theory, and for teaching me the difference between being a human and being a person. You still owe me a game of Sorry! To my wonderful teachers at St. Benedict Elementary school, Mrs. Craver, Mrs. Spizzirri, and Mrs. Humphries, thank you for instilling in me the love of learning. Each one of you made school feel like home; that is a feeling I chase to this day, as I am never as at home as much as when I'm in the classroom. To my St. Peter Claver Church family, thank you for showing me that the word family is not limited to blood relations. Thank you for assisting my parents in providing my siblings and I with a nurturing environment full of examples of what it's like to be a kind human. The love and support you have provided us over the years is indescribable. You all *are* family. To my maternal first cousins, the Mildred crew! The bond we all have is insane. We are cousins, but we grew up like siblings. All the laughter, tears, fights trained me to go out into the world and face it. We may not talk as often

Acknowledgments

as we would like to, but every time we come together, we pick
right back up where we left off. There is no family on earth
like ours, and I love y'all to death! To my aunts and uncles on
both sides, thank you for always encouraging me to be smart
even when it wasn't "cool." Thank you for always showing
me love and being an inspiration. Again, there is no family on
earth like ours! Last, but certainly not least, I thank my grandmothers Mildred Davis and Birdetta Palmer for being strong
women who led by example. Neither of you led easy lives, but
you wouldn't know it. Both of you were women the world had
never seen, and I doubt will ever see again. I wish you could
see me now, but I know you always knew what was possible...
long before I did!